CIRCLING BACK

Am. West

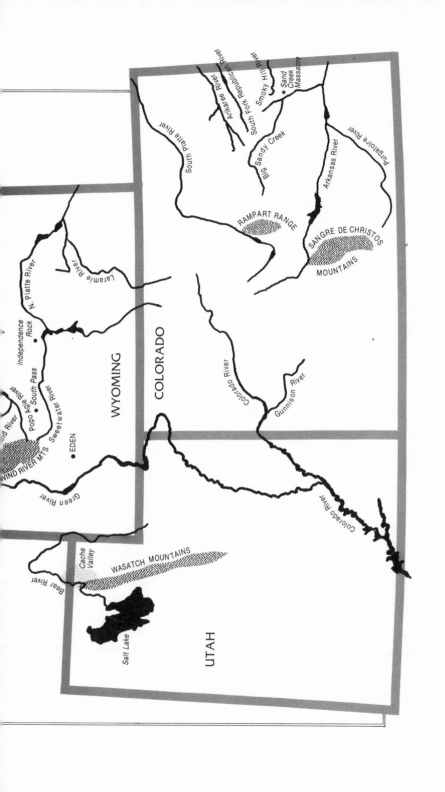

CIRCLING BACK

GARY H. HOLTHAUS

➜P

GIBBS M. SMITH, INC.
PEREGRINE SMITH BOOKS
SALT LAKE CITY
1984

Copyright © 1984 by Gibbs M. Smith, Inc.

No part of this book may be used or reproduced in any
manner without prior written consent from the publishers.

Published by Gibbs M. Smith, Inc.
Peregrine Smith Books
P.O. Box 667, Layton, UT 84041

First edition

Library of Congress Cataloging in Publication Data

Holthaus, Gary H., 1932-
    Circling Back
    "Peregrine Smith Books"
    Bibliography
    1. West (U.S.)—History—Poetry.   I. Title.
PS3558.043L3   1984   813'.54   83-20136

Book Design by J. Scott Knudsen
Manufactured in the United States of America

TABLE OF
CONTENTS

*I*n those days, the land Shubur-Hamazi,
Harmony-tongued Sumer, the great land . . .
*Uri, the land having all that is appropriate,
The land Martu, resting in security,
The whole universe, the people well cared for
To Enlil in one tongue gave speech.*

*Then the lord defiant, the prince defiant, the king
      defiant,
Enki, who scans the land . . .
Changed the speech in their mouths, put contention
      into it,
Into the speech of man that (until then) had been
      one."*

     Sumerian poem

*N*ot I but the world says it:
All is one."

     Herakleitos
     fragment 118

*I*n the beginning all was Brahman,
One and infinite. . . . He who is in
*The sun, and in the fire and in the
Heart of man is One. . . . He is ever
One, he is ever One."*

     Maitri Upanishad
     fragments 6.17 and 2.7

*C*ome now, I will first tell you of the
beginning, from which all the things
*we now look upon came forth into view: Earth, and
the sea with many waves, and damp Air, and the
Titan Aether which clasps the circle all round."*

     Empedocles
     fragment 38

INTRODUCTION

WHY RETELL THE STORY OF THE AMERICAN WEST? There are personal reasons. When I began this, my son, Kevin, was hunting and trapping the Yellowstone River in the very places the mountain men, the people of Plenty-Coups and Crazy Horse, the soldiers of Custer and Crook, hunted, trapped, fought, suffered and worked out their lives. My daughter, Stephanie, was attending Rocky Mountain College in Billings. "Rocky Mountain College" is the name Jim Bridger, Osborne Russell, Joe Meek and their friends gave their encampment near the Yellowstone in the winter of 1835. There they passed the time reading aloud to one another and in argument and debate, and there, Russell reported, "Some of my comrades who considered themselves Classical scholars have had some little added to their wisdom." The closeness, continuity and availability of history seem very near under such circumstances, and its circular rather than linear aspects seem more clear. So I want to retell this for myself and my family, trying to make a unified story out of the land and the many events that mark the place where we lived important years together.

There are other, broader reasons as well. At some point, perhaps not in any time or place we know, but in the deep recesses of our human intuition, we were all one people. Altamira, though wrong in time, may serve as metaphor for that. Out of the earth, the caves, we came, some of us moving slowly eastward across the steppes, through Siberia, across a land bridge to America, our experience becoming history, legend, myth, shaping our values and world views. Others of us moved west. Through Greece and Rome and Trafalgar Square we came, across the Atlantic to America. Our western experience created a different history, legend, myth, and shaped different values and world views. We came together again, members of the same family, in this new place and after many years, our differing experiences making recognition impossible and conflict inevitable. The final working out of that conflict continues into our own day, but the story of our coming together again lies in our plains and mountains, and in the stories that survive us. It is an important, disturbing and tragic story whose substance is both elusive and attractive, drawing us to it again and again.

One value of stories is that they provide a vehicle for talking about things beyond the stories themselves. We are people of the word—word as creative act, and word as bond. Stories become the means of exploring our bonds, the agreements we make with ourselves, with one another and with the earth. They may expand our vision, allowing us to see more than we have before, or they may narrow our view, providing both depth and focus for our perception of the world. They illumine the sacredness and madness, the meaning and lack of it, in our connections with one another, and with all creatures animate or inanimate.

There is a peculiar unity (peculiar only because we have become accustomed to seeing life in dichotomies or myriad fragments) to all creation. This notion is reflected in both eastern and western thinkers as we move back in time towards our common roots. Pre-Socratics and Zen priests appear to share a common view of the "earth breathing in, breathing out;" a single organism which, like an animal or an ecosystem, is affected in every part when touched in any part. They seem to foreshadow the old Sioux song, "We are all related; we are all one," and tell us we cannot harm or disrespect any part of the whole without ultimately harming, and revealing our disrespect for, ourselves. Stories are one means of exploring such an idea.

Further, some stories are never told once and for all. "What is right," says Empedocles, "can well be uttered even twice." We create stories, but the great stories last, and return to create us. They go out and come back. We retell them and send them out again. How do we speak of friends, of those we love, or warn ourselves of those we fear, except through stories? The story becomes the medium for life itself. The old ones gone continue to tell us how to live through stories. Those stories with the substance of myth must be told over and over again in each generation.

Without a story the present is less sensible and less bearable, the future more difficult to discern and more frightening. In the great stories of any people we are nourished, revealed to ourselves, inspired by the deeds of heroes, brought to the edge of despair by the shadow that falls "between the idea and the reality." But the past, put before us in a story, is at the same time put behind us, and we are healed. The story is our refuge; its respite enables a new freedom in us: past and present are commingled, and the outlines of the future, though vague, are made visible, for the seeds of the past we may be sure, are growing into the present and will ripen, fall into history, and grow again in the days to come.

The settling of the American West is the story of a past that continues to haunt us, assaulting the present in lingering racial tensions and hostility, and in policy questions that remain unresolved or recur with alarming regularity. Where is justice to be found in Indian claims to land or water? How do we resolve the disputes about who has what authority on a reservation? What land policies will best serve agriculture, industry and the land itself? There are no answers to such questions here. But, "insofar as any 'mastering' of the past is possible," writes Hannah Arendt, "it consists in relating what has happened. . . . The poet in a very general sense and the historian in a very special sense have the special task of setting the process of narration in motion and involving us in it." But even when the poet and the historian have done their best, the past can never be wholly overcome or undone. "The best that can be achieved," she concludes, "is to know precisely what it was, and to endure this knowledge, and then to wait and see what comes of knowing and enduring."

America has hardly had distance enough to know the story wholly, nor time enough to endure it; the story needs to be told over and over, even with tongues too feeble to tell it all. It is not important to learn immediately the meaning of events; it is important that the meaning is there for the learning, sometimes to be recognized much later. One value of the story and the retelling of it is that it keeps the meaning alive, and available for us when the future requires it. It then offers us a hope of renewal, for these old stories ask us to create something new, to fulfill our commitments, to be more than we have been willing to be.

This effort, then, is one attempt to bring disparate elements – symbols and events from our mutual life and history – together in a story that enables me to find some order in them and in my own life, to organize ideas and events of the past so the present makes more sense and the future is more hopeful. These symbols and ideas are not entirely from the western landscape or western thought. Somehow, soon I hope, both western and eastern thought must regain something of that commonality they once had. A story may help us toward that end.

The story begins with the land, for invaders – from the first hunters to cross the Bering land bridge to the most recent settlers – encountered in the western landscape an immensity unimaginable without personal experience of it. In so doing they also encountered themselves and were forced thereby to reconsider their heritage and their values as well. And it is the land that knits the story whole. This is as it should be, for whether Red Man or White, our roots lie, not in some home town elsewhere, not in England or Europe, nor across a land bridge from Siberia, nor yet in ancient Greece or the old way of Folsom man. Beyond and behind those places and those times there is a mutuality in our human joy and pain, and in them the old song is fulfilled: "We are all related, we are all one." The root lies deep, not in some distant time or culture, but in the earth herself. We may destroy ourselves warring over her, but we are *of* the earth.

The West of the Rockies, and the plains that lift us to them, is the land upon which much of America's most exciting past was acted out. The earth here is as much the source of our national character and experience as are Plymouth and Jamestown. Whether emigrant or stay-at-home, the West was *the* experience for us all, and its history binds us together more strongly than other forces tear us apart. I was privileged to live there for a time; no other place will ever seem so much like home. Perhaps this will be a way of saying thanks to the people, and the land, that make it so.

G. H. H.

ACKNOWLEDGEMENTS

THIS RETELLING IS NOT AN EFFORT TO SEE THE WEST in an epic dimension. Rather its purpose is to tell the story of large events through the use of small details. To say thousands of Indians died of smallpox in the 1830s tells us something, but to tell the story of Little Dog and the smallpox reveals something else. So these retellings are more in the nature of an anthology or, better, a mosaic; many small events juxtaposed in order to establish the larger contours of an era. The sources are historic documents, journals, records, or reports of early observations of Indians, or stories I have been told. I have tried to select from these the most revealing of the lives and character and circumstances in which people of the early West worked out their destinies. The other criteria for inclusion were that each piece work toward a sense of wholeness, fit within a narrative structure, and have this particular region as its setting. Because they echo older histories, these little stories, I hope, tell a story larger than the sum of its parts, meant to be read like a novel that may remind us about the land and events that have made us who we are, "relating what has happened," and thus, "setting the process of narration in motion and involving us in it," once again. If we know this story, perhaps something will come from our knowing and enduring.

Many others have told these stories and told them well. Their work is essential and appreciated, and I have used it freely and in various fashions. The Joe Meek stories, for example, are from Frances Fuller Victor's *The River of the West*; all I have done is rearrange them. Other selections, such as the Osborne Russell material, and the stories in the "We Are All Related" section are paraphrases or excerpts simply relined. Throughout I have used the original words or phrases, trying to retain as much of their flavor, individuality and perspective as possible. Some sections, such as the "Report of the Commission," or "West of the Missouri," are made of the actual words, edited and with new line breaks, while some are left in their original prose. The "letters" from Arnold in the "Sound of the Snapping Guidon," are an obvious invention to enable the inclusion of more information about army life on the frontier than any single soldier could have known. The "Prairie Fire" section is from the *Record of Engagements with Hostile Indians*,

1868-1882, General Sheridan's report from the Department of Missouri. The Sand Creek material is from the Congressional records as pulled together by Lewis. The Little Big Horn is from Camp, Ricker, and Graham, recollections of participants generally edited only for brevity, for these are all their stories, not mine; they seem to me to belong together, and I have tried to put them together in a way that provides a kind of unity true to them and to this story. Among the broader histories Robert Utley's remarkable books on the frontier army and the Indian wars, Don Rickey's *Forty Miles a Day on Beans and Hay*, and Alvin Josephy, Jr.'s perceptive treatments of Indian life and history were all invaluable. In recent years the publishing activities of both the University of Nebraska Press and the University of Oklahoma Press have brought many documents once difficult of access into easy reach.

The materials that may appear to be Indian are non-Indian observations of Indians, or they are stories translated for Whites by Indians. The point is important for they are always an approximation only, and reflect both the strengths and flaws of such viewpoints. It seems wiser to use such material rather than try to put oneself into an Indian psyche, or use material that is more properly the terrain of Indians themselves.

This is not a scholarly paper, and there has been no effort to use footnotes. I think in every case the source of the material can be found in the title or within the story. Obviously many good sources have not been selected. I hope that has been more by design than by ignorance. A list of sources has been included at the end. Uncited (or unsightly) material is the author's responsibility.

A number of people have read the early drafts of this manuscript and offered comments on it. Kenneth Brewer, Drummond Hadley, David Hansen, Carolyn and Robert Hedin, Geary Hobson, Stan Jenkins, Michael Kennedy, Tom Lyon, Frederick Manfred, Dorik Mechau, Martha Montgomery, Richard Nelson, William Schneider, Gary Snyder, Robert Utley, Richard Vollertson, Vern Waples, Carla Van West, and Keith Wilson have all offered encouragement. Special thanks to my wife, poet Nancy Hill McCleery, who not only read it all, but listened to much of it too, and who willingly turned me loose to work on it. Comments and criticisms from these folks have contributed to whatever strength it may have. Any failures of language, conception, or history are my own.

This book is for them, and for those old friends who make the West such a rich place to be.

G. H. H.

CIRCLING BACK

I. PRELUDE

*To think and to be
are one and the same."*
Parmenides
fragment iii

*This universe is a trinity
and this is made of name,
form, and action. Those three
are one."*
Brihad-Aranyaka
Unpanishad 1.6

*Between the conception
And the creation
Between the emotion
And the response
Falls the shadow*

Life is very long

*"Between the desire
And the spasm
Between the potency
And the existence
Between the essence
And the descent
Falls the shadow."*
T. S. Eliot
"The Hollow Men"

CONTEXTS:
THE BEGINNING

At the beginning
Before Christ was—
        Before Coyote!—
Before Raven stole light from its box
Or Wolf nursed the boisterous twins,
Before the first dawn or first evening
Or oldest man's oldest thought,
Before mountains or rivers,
Before the power of the word
        to open up the world

Before all that—
Moving through the vast silence
There was number, pulse,
Numbers ordering themselves in time
Becoming time made tangible
Becoming
Music and word
Form and formation
        of ourselves.

Without music
Word is not complete
The form is not comely.

Without word
Idea is but a part,
The formation is not complete.

Out of music
And the word
Came life,
        the single, rhythmic line
        along the backs of buffalo at Lascaux,
        the antelope painted by Bushmen
        on the rock walls above the Veldt,
        the medicine shields of the Crows
        in the Cottonwood country.

Out of music and the word
Everything that was to come
Came.

The first music to come
Was a song.
It had the power of songs
To give the world a comely form.
The first song was
      The Creation.

The first word to come
Was a name.
It had the power of names
To become us.
The first word was
      The People.

II. CHANT THE CREATION

W ithout time
Nothing can come into being.
Without place
A thing will certainly not
Come into being.
And without motion
Nothing comes into existence
Or goes out of existence.

Without motion
There is no art."
     Seneca, letter LXV

H ere is the origin of what was,
Is, and will be, The budding of trees
Of men and women,
Beasts and birds and waterspawned fish . . .
Everything breathing in, breathing out;
All creatures with a share of scent
     and breath,
Intelligence and a share of thought."
     Empedocles, excerpts
     fragments 21, 100, 102, 110

T here is this desire:
    Time, motion and music
In the word
A language like liquid . . .

A river,
Yellowstone or Big Horn"
     G. H. H.

CHANT THE CREATION

I

Now
In this high place
Let time and motion meet,
Let music and the word
Come together from the silence.

On Rampart Range
We take our stand
And look through time
Six hundred million years,
The ancestral Rockies
Stirring under a paleozoic sea,

And look
Two hundred million years,
The great trees of Montana
Falling into the green
Sylvanian swamps
Becoming coal
Where the old stone house
In Bearcreek
Now settles in the sagebrush
And the sand.

Stand with me
And watch this creation,
I call you back to me
And to this high place
On Rampart Range;
I do this for you
For I am Earth;
      I was before Atum,
      Before Re
      In his first appearances,
      Before Nun, the encircling
      River. I am Sky before sky,
      River before rivers,
      Older than Apsu the begetter,
      Or Na-pi, the Old Man,
      Older than mountains or plains.
Before anything stepped forth
To receive its name,
I was here,

"Perfectly balanced and poised,"
Between the darkness
And the light.

Now
I show this to you
That you will know
I am Center
And Source of all,
    "What was, is, and will be,"
And I have burned a long time
With this passion, am still aflame
Inside. The heat boils at my center,
Erupts on my skin,
A great cretaceous outburst;
The fault-block Wasatch rise,
The Grand Tetons,
The fold-belt Rockies heaving up,
The Pryors lifting from their mesozoic sleep,
The Absarokas of Wyoming,
The Crazies of Montana,
Their great volcanic bulk
Spilling over the prairie,
The precambrian Belts with fossil
Seaweed, no fossil animals anywhere,
And south of Judith Basin
The sedimentary Snowies rising,
And south of them
The basement gneiss and granite
Of the Beartooths, seventy million years old,
Their topmost sedimentary layers now
Washed away to Laurel, holding up
The Owl Cafe, Open All Night;
All the basement rocks thrust up behind us,
The upthrust sediments washing down
Great fans of alluvial debris
Creating the plains below us, the topsoil;
The miocene grasses, the grammas, becoming source
For our daily bread,
The pliocene pines and poplars taking hold,
The pleistocene spruce and alders,
All the roots mingling under the topsoil,
Holding the soil, the water;
The dry grass stirring

As the sea stirs, wave after wave
Of movement, the whole prairie breathing
In . . . out . . .

Watch this life
Unfolding before us, for
I am Earth
And I give this to you:
      To see through time
      To see this place in motion
      Coming into being
      The People of all kinds
            four leggeds and two leggeds
            fish people and bird people
All coming . . .

II

Now
From this high place on Rampart Range
Look north through time
See the blue ice
Palm down on the pleistocene pole,
Long fingers of ice reaching south;

Their own weight
Strangling the glaciers of oxygen,
Pressing them blue.

And far below us,
Down the ice free corridors
Where the land emerged as the water fell,
See
A movement—two hunters
Small, tentative against the ice,
Their long spears balanced;
At night one small spark
Against the dark, a drift of smoke . . .

A slow movement of people,
Descendants of my lover Grandfather,
The Hard Blue Sky,
Moving eastward to become
The high plains hunters on foot;
From Folsom, Sandia, Eden Valley they range,
Becoming stalkers and farmers,

Orators and engineers,
Their sleek American technology
Creating the slender fluted point from Folsom;

Moving inexorable as time
Out of silence and the cold,
The pleistocene settlers on this new land,
Mastodons and moropus feeding together,
Sabretooths and more settlers,
All with
        "a share of scent and breath . . .
            intelligence and a share of thought,"
The gray-boned dinosaurs of Montana
        (the same in Mongolia!)
Brachiosaurus asleep in the jurassic limestone
Under the ice.

III

You who believe
We rise from the sea,
Listen:
There are others
Who know
We walked
Up from the center,
Out of the Earth came
Walking the high plains and deserts
Toward the gathering and hunting and learning,
        the adoption of dogs and the learning;
Learning the slender symmetry of points
        from Agate Basin and Brown's Valley,
        the transverse flaking
        from Scottsbluff and Cody and Eden,
        obsidian flakes lodged in the broken ribs
        of animals, falling toward the future
        on the canyon floor;
Learning the coiled pots and shaped pots
        the stamped designs and incised designs,
        the tempering and burning;
Learning the baskets of grass plaited
        so close they hold water for boiling,
Learning to drop the fired stones;
All of us learning,

Becoming
The high plains hunters on horseback;

> Out of the Earth
> We come
> Out of our music
> Our memory
> Out of the word
> We come

Smoke choking the valleys now
But still coming

Learning the movement of animals
>   growing of plants
>   turning of seasons
>   the Sacred Circle, pattern for all
>>   laying it out in pale stones
>>   above the Big Horns
>>   for us all to see;

Learning the rites:
>   Healing
>   Purification
>   Renewal of Arrows
>   Atonement for Exiles

Learning the songs,
>   the drums and dances
>   against the cold

Coming to know this place
>   and our place in it

Learning our way
>   back to the Center
All one and walking
>   "the pathless ways
>   toward home."

THE YELLOWSTONE

"Language is entirely inadequate to convey a just conception of the awful grandeur and sublimity of this masterpiece of nature's handiwork; and in my brief description I shall confine myself to the bare facts."
        Charles M. Cook
        September 21, 1869

Now
The river.

Look north from this high place
To the Yellowstone
Sinuous in a thousand hills,
Carving dark caves and runs
Under the cutbanks,
Beauty and treachery swirling
In the shifting currents,
Gravel sloughing away
From the feet of men or horses,
Buffalo drowning
Crossing the thin ice
In early winter.

Move upstream in the mind,
Past the O'Fallon, the Powder,
The Tongue, the Rosebud waiting to bloom,
Past Pompey's Pillar and Pryor Creek,
The pish-kin in the rims
Where Billings will someday
Rear up from the river
Beyond any white/red
Dream of civilization,
Up that branch flowing in from the south
Where it swings southeast
In a great arc out of the box canyon,
Follow the river falling
From the Sunlight Meadows
Far above—

There, at the bottom of the box,
Turn back, downstream now,
Out of the blind canyon—

Leave it for Joseph escaping the army,
For ranchers and duck hunters, for
This is the Clark Fork of the Yellowstone now;
To the west, a drainage beyond these mountains
Lies the creek named by Hubbel:
        "It was a Hell-Roarer!"
He said,
And on the ridges above see
The shadows of elk
Feeding on Sheridan Creek and Silver Run.

Keep moving in the mind
Down below Line Creek and Gold Creek
Sugarloaf Butte and Grove Creek,
Past the places of towns to come —
Clark, Belfry, Bridger,
Fromberg, Edgar —
The hot springs at Silesia,
The dry towns in their summer heat
Or the beet farmers working their fields
In March when the open winters
Let it happen;

Down past the mouth of Rocky Fork
Now Rock Creek, at whose mouth
        "Howell was shot by two fusee balls
        thro. the chest . . . rode within half a mile
        of camp, fell and was brought in on a litter.
        He lived about twenty hours and expired
        in the greatest agony imaginable."

Turn west again, on the Yellowstone,
Dropping the names on the streams
As you go, the deep-pooled Stillwater,
East Rosebud and West Rosebud
Flowing into it, curving down from the face
Of the Beartooths, where the summer storms hang
Their gray-white cumulus above the canyons,
Past the slick rock bottom of the Boulder,
The Sweetgrass, many rivers flowing north
And east from this high country,
Only Twenty-Five Yard River, now the Shields,
Sliding down from the Crazies toward the south.

The great Missouri calls them,
Yellowstone and all,
Pulling them down;
They move into her
Gentlest and smoothest
Of lovers.

At the great bend
Where the Yellowstone flows
Down from the south, turn—
Up the broad valley where Livingston
Will be, sculpins hiding under the rocks,
Rainbows and cutthroats easy in the pools,
Elk in the bottomland in winter, the mountains
Pearl white at dawn, their long blue shadows
Falling in the hot springs at Chico,
Past the antelope feeding above the river
At Gardiner,
Past the great hot springs at Mammoth
Climb toward the divide
Where east and west shatter,
Fall apart in the clear air.

Lewis and Clark missed all this.
"Old Gabe" Bridger could show us
If he were here now.
Colter saw it too,
Came at it from another way,
Could show us all our past
And future too
If he weren't so tired,
Lay down in his midwest farm fields
To rest forever in the loam.

Cook would see it:
        "A scene of transcendent beauty,"
He said,
        "We could not contain
        our enthusiasm.
        With one accord we all took off
        our hats and yelled
        with all our might."

A scene
You can still see
Past the chemical works,

The buffalo meadows
Where Old Bill Hamilton walked,
Among the first to be there
But unable to tell it he said,
  "Because the outside world
  would not believe stories
  told by trappers
  of the grand and romantic
  scenery to be found
  in the Rocky Mountains.
  Had this wonderland been described
  in St. Louis in the early '40s
  the reply would have been
  'Old Mountaineer's story!' "

You can see it there
In the same place Cook shifted in his saddle,
  "Seeing what appeared to be
  an opening in the forest ahead,"
He presumed it
  "to be a park, or open country."
While his attention was attracted
By the pack animals
Which had paused to eat grass,
His saddle horse suddenly stopped.
He turned forward again and looked
Straight down
  "from the brink of a great canyon,"
The Grand Canyon of the Yellowstone
Gutting the whole country,
Laying it open as an elk carcass
Lays open, field dressed in the snow.
  "I sat there in amazement,"
He wrote,
  "while my companions came up . . .
  It was five minutes before anyone spoke."

And still
The great falls spill
Down the light volcanic rock
To the roaring canyon floor,
The river then, flowing north,
  "A strong brown god,"
Says Eliot,

"Sullen, untamed and intractable,
Patient to some degree. . . ."

This river belongs
        to time and The People coming
For I have given it:
        I am Earth
        Center and Source of all

Sworling out of Canyon
        the past we do not know
                washes down to meet us

Tumbling through Yankee Jim
        the future we cannot see
                pours down upon us

Curling below Spring Creek
        the present we do not understand
                eddies around us

Taking us through time
This river moves within us
        carrying my life
        the lives of The People
        carving
        the dark bones of the land.

III WE ARE ALL RELATED

*A*lways think of the universe as one living organism, with a single substance and a single soul; and observe how all things are submitted to the single perceptivity of this one whole, all are moved by its single impulse, and all play their part in the causation of every event that happens. Remark the intricacy . . . the complexity . . ."

     Marcus Aurelius
     Meditations
     Book Four, 40

*F*ix your mind's eye steadily on things that are absent as though they were present. You will find you cannot distinguish being from being."

     Parmenides
     fragment iii

O You, Power, there where the sun goes down
We are related.
O You, Power, where the Giant lives
We are related.
O You, Power, where the sun comes from
We are related.
O You, Power, there where we always face
We are related.
We are all related
We are all one!"

     Oglala
     "Making Relatives Song"

THE SIOUX

These were the Sioux,
As Denig tells it,
And these their numbers . . .
1833

Teton Sioux
    Se chong hhos 500 lodges
    Ogallalahs 300 lodges
    Min ne con zus 260 lodges
    Se ah sap pas 220 lodges
    Wo hai noom pah 100 lodges
    Honc pap pas 150 lodges
    Etas epe cho 100 lodges

Yancton Sioux
    Lower Yancton 300 lodges
    Pah Baxah 250 lodges
    Wahzecoatai 100 lodges
    Gens des Perches 50 lodges
    Esan tees 30 lodges

These were the heroes of the Sioux:
    Mau-Kaú-Tó-Jan-Joh, the Clear Blue Earth
    Mah-Ghah-Ska, the Swan
    Hai-Wa-Ze-Chah, La Corne Seule, the One Horn
    Ma-To-Tchi-Cah, the Little Bear
    Mau-To-To-Pah, the Four Bears
    Wah-Na-Ton, the Animal Who Rushes
    Wahh-Pai-Sha, the Red Leaf
    Hah-Sas-Hah, the Ioway

And these their ways:
    MAU-KAU-TO-JAN-JOH, the CLEAR BLUE EARTH
    Chief of the Se chong hhos.
    Governed wisely and well,
    Kept his people in order,
    Regulated their hunts.
    His people never starved;
    Pawnee and Arikara scalps
    In great number
    Were brought to his camp.
    These were the qualities of
    Mau-Kaú-Tó-Jan-Joh
    Who gained his reputation
    As a leader loyal to the tribe.

Then came these warriors
Who could handle lance and shield
Who were fast as antelope
Whose hearts were white bears
Whose minds were like elk:

MAH-GHAH-SKA, the SWAN
    Chief of the Ogallalahs.
    Good warrior,
    Sensible leader,
    Man of many talents.

HAI-WA-ZE-CHAH, LA CORNE SEULE, the ONE HORN
    Chief of the Min ne con zus.
    Killed buffalo on foot,
    Attacking with his knife.
    When his wife died
    He announced his own death,
    Went out on the prairie alone
    Put his knife into a great bull,
    Was gored himself,
    Followed his wife to the Place Above.

MAU-TO-TO-PAH, the FOUR BEARS
    Chief of the Two Kettles
    Who makes his people behave.
    A moderate man
    His people war but a little distance,
    They hunt well, never hunger.

And then came

WAH-NA-TON, the ANIMAL WHO RUSHES
    Chief who kept together three camps—
    The Tête Coupées, Gens des Perches, and Gens des Pins,
    Four hundred lodges in all.
    When he died they split the blankets.
    His sense of justice was like this:

        1836
        Some of his band stole
        Six horses from Mr. Dixon, a sutler.
        That fall the bands came back to trade
        Rich with robes and meat.
        Before any exchange could begin
        WAH-NA-TON, Animal Who Rushes,

> Who makes his people behave
> Asked of Dixon a bill
> For the loss of his horses.

It was estimated in buffalo robes.

> Then WAH-NA-TON, politic and sensible,
> Caused all the robes to be brought;
> Everyone brought every robe—
> The Crow Necklace, Black Stone, Who Jumps High,
> Everyone brought to the pile the robes
> From the hunt.

> WAH-NA-TON, shrewd and just,
> Pulled from the pile robes enough
> To pay for the horses,
> Pulled them out without regard for innocence
> Or guilt, making the innocent pay
> As well as the scoundrels, for the onus on them all.
> No warrior complained;
> Each selected from what remained
> If any, of his robes, and began the trade
> As if nothing had happened.

> By such examples as these
> WAH-NA-TON brought his people
> To respect his orders
> And by killing one or two
> To fear his vengeance.

There were also

> WAHH-PAI-SHA, the RED LEAF
> Chief of the Tête Coupées after Wah-Nah-Tah,
> He was variable
> In his attitude toward the whites.

HA-SAS-HAH, the IOWAY
> Chief of the Yanctons.
> His people were well supplied with meat.
> He was impartial in distribution of annuities.
> His whole attention was directed
> To the welfare of his people.

These were the men of the Sioux
As Denig told it,
And these were their ways.
The strength of their names

Caused the Sioux to be known throughout the plains
And laid the dread of them upon all nations.

THE CHEYENNES

SHA-HAI-YEN-NA
The People of Alien Speech

*"There is no finer race of men than these in all North America and none
superior in stature, except the Osages: scarcely a man in the tribe full grown
who is less than six feet in height."*
    George Catlin

After the farming, the soil
Turning to blood in their hands,
After the move from Minnesota,
The subjugation in Oklahoma,
The winter of escape, the last days
Above Hat Creek, their blood in the snow,
The subjugation again . . .

Tsis-tsis-tas, they called themselves
The People.

Proud
Handsome
Fearless
Well-dressed
Famed for their horses and their horsemanship,
The beauty and chastity of their women,
The prowess and bravery of their warriors

Hoebel wrote of them:

This tribe is a cluster
Of Arrows. An arrow alone
May be broken; bound together
The Arrows are strong.

If one Cheyenne
Kills another Cheyenne,
The Arrows are polluted.
So long as they are soiled
Bad times will stalk The People.
Blood revenge and feuding
Are not the Cheyenne Way.
They do not offer compensation

To a victim's kin,
For such a deed offends them all
And threatens the strength
Of everyone.

The People know
A murderer soils himself.
He rots inside and his body begins
To stink. Therefore
The symbols of the mutual life—
Eating from the common bowl,
Smoking the ritual pipe—
Are forbidden.

Lesser people seek revenge.
In the Cheyenne way
Banishment is best
For such offense,
Exile and provision of a dream,
A dream of renewal.

These are beliefs
That make Cheyenne hearts large,
And these the rituals
That restore unity and purity
To the tribe:

If one who has killed behaves properly
In every way,
After three, five, ten years
He may be taken back, the dream
Of renewal fulfilled,
If the relatives of the victim consent.

Then the Arrow Renewal
Will be undertaken,
The murderer restored,
The tribe made whole again.

Atonement and Purification of Arrows
Accomplish this. Nothing else
Enables it.

THE COURAGE OF TWO-TWISTS

In 1821, Paul Kane writes,
Two-Twists, a Cheyenne,
Vowed to drive the Crows
From their breastworks
And die a warrior's noble death.

He charged the Crows alone
Other Cheyennes all watching—
Charged alone!
Armed with a sabre only!
He could not be brought down,
Fought furiously
Right into the Crow camp!

His fellow warriors were stirred;
They joined the charge,
The fortress was broken,
Everyone in the camp was captured
Or killed.

THE CONICAL CAP

George Engler heard it
From Old Man Howse who told it
This way, then laughed.

> We was out huntin'
> Come up behind
> This old Cheyenne buck
> Asleep, his head on a log.

> All we could see, really,
> Was one a them conical caps
> They used to wear, made outta
> Buffalo hide, yuh know.
> Winter cap. You've seen 'em.

> Well, we just decided
> To see if we could surprise him some,
> Put a ball through the top
> Of his hat don' cha know.

We were fair close
So Tom took a good bead
And touched her off . . .

Now wouldn'tcha know—
His head come further up in that cone
Than you woulda thought!

HOW THE CHEYENNES RECEIVED CORN AND BUFFALO

Way Seger heard it
And told it
One Indian dove headfirst
Into the spring.
The other Indian followed.
They came out together
Where an old woman was
Baking bread.
The old woman asked,
 "Why have you come?"

She seated one at her left
The other at her right
And asked them this,
 "Why have you come?"

They said,
 "Our people are starving.
 The Great Spirit told us to come here.
 An old woman would tell us what to do."

The old woman said,
 "I know all about it.
 I have prepared something for you
 And for your people
 To eat."

She showed them a field of corn
Wide as the eye could see.
She showed them a herd of buffalo
Wide as the eye could see.
She taught them to plant corn,
She taught them to kill buffalo.
She taught them to make bread of the corn,
She taught them to dress the buffalo.
She gave them quantities of both
To take back with them.

She said,
> "Feed the men first,
> They have to hunt so that others may eat.
> Feed the women next,
> They have to cook so that others may eat.
> Feed the children and the orphans next
> And all those who are dependent
> Until all are satisfied."

The men swam up through the spring
And returned home.
The buffalo came out of the spring after them.
The people planted the corn and tended it
And lived on it through the winters
When the buffalo drifted south.

THE AGENT WANTS TO TRADE

Seger remembered this:

A Cheyenne chief asked
for a permit to hunt buffalo
off the reservation.

The agent said,
> "Give me your son."

The chief protested,
> "Why should I give you my son?"

"So I can put him in school
> and make a White Man of him."

The chief laughed,
> "Then give me a white boy
> to make an Indian of."

WE WILL TAKE YOUR CHILDREN

White Man says:

> We will take your children
> We will teach them the White Man's road.
> We will keep them away from you
> For months or years.

If they come back to you
You will not know who they are.
They will not know themselves
Who they are.

They will not speak your language
They will be ashamed of your houses
And uncomfortable in your beds.

The young men will not know
How to hunt or endure cold.
The young women will not know
How to sew hides or prepare foods.

The old ways will be rubbed out
With your old people,
The old tribe feeling,
Knowledge of the Circle,
Of Earth, Mother and Grandmother
And of Sky, Father and Grandfather
Power and Mystery,
Will all be gone.

They will forget the Arrow Renewal,
The Sweat Lodge.
They will not cry for a Vision
Nor make sacrifices in the Sun Dance.

You and your children will not be able
To speak to one another;
Your fathers will not be able to speak
To your sons,
Your mothers will not be able to speak
To your daughters,
Your children will have no respect
For your fathers or your mothers
Or for you.

After a short time
They will turn away,
Your head will always be down;
You will have no one to help
In the tribal rituals,
You will have no one to help
In your old age.
The young will turn away.

We call this education, they say,
It will be good for your children.
We will make your young civilized,
They will walk the White Man's road.

TRIBES ARE LIKE WAVES

Seger recalls an old man saying:
". . . tribes of people are like waves of the ocean which roll along until it
strikes the shore then it vanishes, but another wave takes its place
and follows it until it too strikes the shore, when it also vanishes, so
it will be with the tribes of people, one tribe follows another, when
one tribe passes away, another takes its place, and it will be so until
eternity. . . ."

THE CROWS

". . . *the Crow. This nation is distinguished for bravery and skill in war.*"
    James Ohio Pattie

In the beginning
Were "The People."
Absaroka and Hidatsa were one,
And together.
Their great hunters
Drove the shaggy heads of buffalo
Into the arms of The People,
The cut arms of The People,
Standing open like a human fence,
A great V of them
Narrowing over the bluff . . .
The beasts a brown river of hide,
Flesh straining, throats bellowing,
The terrible tumbling into a broken heap,
Giving themselves
For the abundance of The People.

Even with this plenty
An Absaroka woman claimed a beast
An Hidatsa claimed also.
They fell into dispute;
Their men came up, the argument grew
As their numbers increased

Until blood was drawn.
Those most aggrieved moved away.

The two maintained the same language,
The common words marked by Traders
For use in their common trade.

Absaroka remains the name:
    bird people, sparrow-hawk.
The Cheyenne call them
    O-e-tún-i-o-, the "Crow People."

Their country was the Yellowstone,
Their power was in visions.
Tobacco was their sacred crop,
Horses were their pride.

Lowie says:
The four great exploits were:
        The touching of an enemy, Dà'kce, or "coup,"
        Snatching away a bow or gun in hand-to-hand combat,
        Theft of a horse picketed in an enemy camp,
        Being the pipe-owner or raid planner.

A "Chief" was any man who
Accomplished at least one of these.

BELL-ROCK was a leader, Lowie says,
        Who excelled on every count:
        Had captured five guns,
        Cut loose two tethered horses,
        Struck six undisputed coups,
        Led eleven war parties,
        Never lost a warrior in combat. . . .

Crows ranged all along the Yellowstone:
North to Musselshell
South to Laramie Fork on the Platte.
The Powder, the Wind, the Big Horn,
The small streams, Rocky Fork, West Fork,
Basin Creek, Line Creek, Blue Water,
The lupine meadows on the flanks
Of Mount Maurice—
All were home to them.

At a Crow camp
On an island in the Yellowstone River
A few miles east of where

Billings now grows
François LaRocque wrote,
> "They told me that in winter they were always to be found at a
> park by the foot of the Mountain a few miles from this or
> thereabouts. In the spring and fall they are upon this River
> (Yellowstone) and in summer upon the Tongue and Horses River."

Horses were their love
And their indulgence.
> "The pattern of Crow horse trading,"
John Ewers says,
> "was well established as early as the first decade of the nineteenth cen-
> tury. They obtained horses, Spanish riding gear and blankets, and horn
> bows from the Flatheads, Shoshones, and Nez Perces farther west in
> exchange for objects of European manufacture (metal knives, awls, spear
> and arrow heads, kettles, ornaments, and a few guns). At the Hidatsa
> villages they traded some of the horses and other articles received from
> the western tribes, together with dried meat, skin lodges, and clothing
> prepared by Crow women, for corn, pumpkins, tobacco, and European
> trade articles."

WE PAINT OUR FACES BLACK

1856
February,
Denig tells,
Blackfeet warriors drive off 70 horses
Early in the night.
This morning
A hundred Crows pursue them.
Each warrior rides one fast horse,
Each warrior leads another fast horse.
> The Blackfeet are far ahead;
> They have to break a road
> Through deep snow; their horses are slowing.
> Three days and two nights
> We keep up the chase.
> The horses tire, we leave them behind.
> At the close of this second day
> Our reserve horses give out!
> We continue on foot.
> During all this time
> In cold, in darkness, in snow

No Crow and no Blackfoot has eaten,
No Crow and no Blackfoot has drunk
Or slept.

"The Crows are perhaps the richest nation in horses of any residing east
of the Rocky Mountains. It is not uncommon for a single family to
be the owner of 100 of these animals. Most middle-aged men have
from 30 to 60. An individual is said to be poor when he does not
possess at least 20. . . . The Blackfeet also have plenty and this is
cause for continual war."

On this evening, our third day out,
The Blackfeet are worn down;
Their bellies rumble.
They do not know we are so near.
They kill a buffalo for a feast.
They are cooking!
We smell the smoke and the odor of meat.
We are faint with hunger but the horses
Are not here!
We hurry on, skirting the Blackfeet camp.
A few miles beyond we find the animals
Where the enemy has left them.
We take them and drive them in the dark
Far below the Blackfeet campfire.
Some wish to attack the camp tonight.
Our leader, wiser than we in the warrior way,
Waits for the break of day.
Everything goes as he foresaw.

At dawn the Blackfeet separate
To find the horses.
Two men follow the tracks
Near where we lie in wait.

We attack these two . . .
One escapes! One tries to fire his gun!
He is too tired to run.
He is stabbed. We scalp him alive,
Cut his body up against the future life.

We have what we have come far to find;
Have killed an enemy
With no loss to ourselves.

> We paint our faces black
> To show the victory,
> Go home with songs.

"Such skirmishes and chases are of daily occurrence summer and winter
around both Crow and Blackfeet camps. During a year more than
100 are killed on each side."

HORSE

At dawn Horse came drinking
Dawn Horse came,
Small as first light before Sun is up
Small as Dog
Dawn Horse came,
With toes instead of hooves,
Nose too heavy, legs too short.

But he sure looked like somebody
Familiar. Perhaps it was
Coyote! In disguise!
Coyote could do that —
Become anything he liked!
Could have been Coyote,
Changing, preening himself,
Becoming Middle Horse,
Letting go those toes,
Growing stronger, independent,
Learning to run and to be
Tricky. Equus.

We thought they all died a while.
Maybe old Coyote died too!
At the same time!
We weren't too sure about it . . .
Coyote is cunning!

But he wasn't dead.
Horse wasn't dead either,
Just gone from this place
For a time.

Maybe Horse is still
Coyote in disguise,
Maybe that's why some horses

Don't get tame even now—
Just stay wild and flame-eyed and pecky.
Ride 'em a ways
All smooth and feeling peaceful
Then BANG
The world unfolds
Before you, everything opening
Wide for an instant,
Sky, ground, horse,
All mixed up!

Then you know
That's old Coyote
Still hanging around from a million years ago
Roaming those big savannahs,
Raising hell,
Showing who's trickiest,
The toughest—
Free or dead, the only choice
For Dawn Horse
Old Coyote.

THE ASSINIBOINS

Who received their name from the Chippewa
"One who cooks by the use of stones."

The Stonies or Stone Indians.

Also Tlú-tlama-eka or "Cutthroats" (Kutenai)
Swanton says.

> "The Assiniboins who reside in the vicinity of this fort, I found
> the most kind and honorable of any tribe that I met with."
>   Denig

> "There are three divisions, viz:"
Says Lowie,
>   "Ho-ke (Like Big Fish)
>   Tu-wá-huda (Looking Like Ghosts)
>   Sitcó-ski (Tricksters, lit. 'Wrinkled Ankles')
>   There are thirteen smaller bands."

Like the rest
They began as one people:

We were all Yanktonai then
But we parted,
Our families moving first
To Lake Winnipeg,
Leaving our home at Lake of the Woods
Leaving Lake Nipigon,
Leaving everything we could not carry.

Later we trekked to the rivers
Called Assiniboin and Saskatchewan
And became allies with the Cree.
The bitterness of our memories was great;
We warred continually
With our relatives to the south.

We knew the White traders and trappers well.
We learned their ways and had many dealings
With those explorers who would bring others.
We were kind to them,
And honest in our way.
They were only a few and we did not mind,
But they became many and intolerable.
Betrayal was their way
Even when they loved us.
They did not know what they were doing
Nor did we
Until it was too late.

François Lucie, a factor, told this to Paul Kane,
    "I had my horses stolen by Assiniboins.
    I caught up with one,
    Sheathed my weapon in his heart.
    The savage did not die immediately
    Although I had ripped his breast
    So open I could see his heart throbbing;
    Yet he never let go of the lasso
    Of my stolen horse
    Till it ceased beating
    Which was for some minutes
    Though I tried to pull it
    From his hand."

We are surrounded by enemies:
The Crow to the south
Blackfeet to the west
Gros Ventres of the Prairie to the northwest

Minnetarres on the east
Sioux on the southeast

Only the Crees are our friends,
Only their road is open to us
When our game is gone.

Nevertheless, bad neighbors make us
Good warriors; our sudden rushes
Are feared by all. When brought to a stand
We will fight, desperately, and without
Quarter.

Denig traded with us often
And knew our difficulties
And our territory well:

> "The chief rivers running through the Assiniboin country are first,
> the Missouri, which needs no description here, next is the Milk
> River, a long narrow stream fordable the year around, except during
> spring thaws or continual rains. It flows a southwest course out of the
> small mountains east of the Missouri. The water at high stage has a
> white and milky appearance."

> "Quaking Asp, Porcupine, Big Muddy, Little Muddy, and Knife
> River also flow through Assiniboin country, but they are of little
> consequence. Also the White Earth River, which takes its name from
> the fine white pipe clay found half way to its head."

Surrounded by enemies
Our greatest enemy was disease.
The Trader's account is best:

1838
Smallpox took away
The White traders at Ft. Union,
Many of them gone under.

When the first band of Assiniboins
Came to trade, they were warned off
But they would not be turned away
And passed on to the fort.

250 lodges, upwards of 1000 souls
Contracted the disease at the same time.
By fall only 30 lodges, 150 persons old and young,
Survived.

Our dead were daily
Thrown into the river by cartloads.
Other bands tried to come in;
The result was always the same.
Many of us died before
Any eruption appeared, always
Accompanied by hemorrhages
From the mouth and ears.

Some tried to run away;
The autumnal roads were lined
With dead and lodges
Sweet with stench.

Little Dog,
After losing his favorite child,
Said to his wife,
        "Let us kill the whole family
        before we are all so disfigured
        we present a disgusting appearance
        in the future world."

His wife agreed to this,
Provided he should kill her first,
As she did not wish to witness
The death of their children.
She said,
        "I trust you to do it all."

Little Dog
Set about his task methodically.
He shot all his horses and dogs,
Shot his wife,
Cut the throats of his two remaining children,
Blew his own brains out.

        What could be done for us was done
        By White medicine and Red.
        Our warriors were bled and died;
        They were purged and died.
        Every care was taken;
        Death was always the result.
        The very old and the very young
        Seemed strongest;
        Our principal men all died.

Of 1000 Assiniboin lodges
That came to trade
That terrible year,
Only 400 remained
After the next winter.

For those who lived
        Kinship patterns were extinguished,
        Property was lost or sacrificed.
        Bands were scattered,
        Leadership was dead.

The remnants
Hunted for one another
Among the scattered bands
Opening the flaps of abandoned
Teepees. . . .

        Our young grew without guidance.
        We had to train new leaders,
        Regain our property.

        "Nevertheless,"
Denig writes,
        "through all these distressing and trying scenes the Indians have
    behaved remarkably well toward the Whites. Although aware they
    were primarily the cause of the disorder being brought among them,
    yet nothing in the way of revenge took place either at the time or
    afterwards."

AN INDIAN SERMON

Paul Kane records
a certain missionary came for the summer.
He brought with him a carat of tobacco for trade.
Should he require them,
he would purchase horses and supplies
for his return trip, and pay for them
with this tobacco.

He was welcomed by the Assiniboin
who immediately inquired
if he had any tobacco
for their stock was exhausted.

But this White Man in a black coat was afraid.
If he acknowledged that he had any
they would want it all,
leaving him nothing to barter.
He denied possession.

He was a kind man and good;
he talked eloquently and many listened
to his word. He visited with them
through the summer and tried to lead
them in his paths of righteousness.

When he was about to return
to his own country
he went to Mah-Min, the Chief,
and told him he needed stores
and horses for his travel.
He would pay for them, he said,
with tobacco.

Mah-Min said to him,
          "You preach to the Indians
          many things;
          you tell them not to steal or lie.
          How can they believe or listen to you?
          You said you have no tobacco
          and now you say you have plenty.
          You are the father of lies."

THE BLACKFEET

Names of the Blackfeet were these:

> Sik-sika, "Blackfeet," so called because of the
> discoloration of moccasins by ashes from prairie fires,
> but more probably their moccasins were died black.

> Ah-hí-tä-pe, former name for themselves, meaning "Blood People."

> Sawketakix, name for themselves meaning "Men of the Plains."

> Pó-o-mas, Cheyenne name meaning "Blankets Whitened with
> Earth."

These were their tribes:

> The Blackfeet, who occupied the northern territory

The Bloods, who lived south of the Blackfeet
The Piegans, who are most numerous in the United States.

These tribes too
Once lived in the east,
Migrated west, were located there
When Lewis and Clark came through.

1849
Paul Kane said,
      "They were the best mounted, the best looking, the most warlike
   in appearance, and the best accoutered of any tribe I had ever seen
   on the continent."

The horse was their life-tie,
Enabled war, allowed them
To destroy their enemies,
Increase their wealth,
Hunt
And range the plains from Canada to Mexico,
From the Rockies to the Platte.

      "The height of pleasure
         to a Blackfoot,"
Says Grinnell,
      "was to ride a good horse."

      "After our smoke,"
Kane tells,
      "several of the young braves
      engaged in a horse race,
      to which sport they are very partial,
      and at which they bet heavily;
      they generally ride on those occasions stark naked,
      without a saddle, and with only a lasso
      fastened to the lower jaw of the horse."

It was desire for the horse
that provoked the travel
of Blackfeet braves,
and the horse that made it
possible. Grinnell says,

      "In the very early days of this century, war parties used commonly
   to start out in the spring, going south to the land where horses were
   abundant, being absent all summer and the next winter, and

returning the following summer or autumn, with great bands of
horses.

Sometimes they were gone for two years. . . ."

BIG SNAKE I

Paul Kane wrote to his friends:

Big Snake heard that one
Had blamed him—

> "He has involved the tribe in much
> inconvenience and destroyed
> our chance to trade,"

was said.

On hearing this
Big Snake
went directly to the one
who had spoken thus of him.

Big Snake was armed
and attempted to stab the man.
His foot slipped, the man was spared
his life, but received a terrible wound
in his side.

The two men continued
in deadly hostility for a long time.

At last Big Snake's friends
Persuaded him to seek peace.

Big Snake went to his enemy's lodge,
but before he went he made certain preparations.
He told his wife,

> "If there is any disturbance
> move this lodge immediately
> to that small hill
> where I might more easily defend it."

Then going to the man's lodge
Big Snake found him
seated inside with his wife,
and his children were about him.
Taking up one of the children

Big Snake spoke to it,
asking the child to intercede
with his father and seek peace.

The man would not acknowledge that he had heard.

Big Snake spoke through the child once more,
    "Take pity on me. Let us end this hatred.
    Now."

The man was moody, he held his head down
so Big Snake could not see his face.
He would not look up at Big Snake, or speak.

Big Snake became enraged.
He had condescended to deal
with this lesser man,
and now this man was making him look
foolish. He was humiliated.

Big Snake rushed from the tent,
seized his gun and fired
through the skins of the lodge.
He killed two,
wounded two more,
then dashed for the hill
where his wife was,
following his instructions.
There he remained.

No one in camp
would touch him or punish him
in any way
so great was the fear
he created in every man.

HUNTING

Grinnell told this of us:
    "When bows and arrows, and later, muzzle-loading 'fukes' were the
    only weapons, no more buffalo were killed than could actually be
    utilized. But after the Winchester repeater came in use, it seemed as if
    the different tribes vied with each other in wanton slaughter. . . . The
    hunters would run as long as their horses could keep up with the
    band, and literally cover the prairie with carcasses, many of which
    were never even skinned."

Which may be true,
but only part —

If it had been guns only . . .
But by the time repeaters came
the whites had brought their new
disease: a Christian view combined
with fierce commerce.
His crafts and cunning seduced us all;
in face of these we cut
the old ties, our ancient
interdependence, animals, plants and men.
It was disease destroyed
both will and means
to keep the old ways live.

We all adapt to fortune
or to fate, and new ways gleam
like new white steel before a fire.
Their guns cut loose the greed
that fit that new religion well
which tells us that to prosper
is the sign we need;
they made the world
seem ours again. Only then
did we, too, cover the earth
with carcasses . . .

BIG SNAKE II

One day Big Snake
rode away by himself
according to Paul Kane,
hoping to find some Cree horses
left behind after a battle.
Since he wished everything
for himself, he went alone.

A Cree chief saw him
riding alone on the plain.

Burning with vengeance
the Cree rushed upon Big Snake
who would not fly
from a single foe,
but galloped boldly forward.

The two men closed;
the fight was brief.
With a lance the chief of the Cree
pierced Big Snake's chest
at their first pass.
He was scalped and dead
in an instant.

LIFE SONG

I make this dance
an offering to you
Earth
that my feet may be light
upon the way.

I make this silence
an offering to you
Sky
that my mind may be clear
upon the way.

I make this amulet
an offering to you
The Four Winds
that I may roam everywhere
yet always be in my place
upon the way.

I make my life
an offering to each of you
The Four Directions
that I may not be lost
upon the way.

IV. SO VAGRANT A CONDITION

A strange, wild, terrible, romantic, hard, and exciting life they lead, with alternate plenty and starvation, activity and repose, safety and alarm, and all the other adjuncts that belong to so vagrant a condition, in a harsh, barren, untamed, and fearful region of desert, plain, and mountain. Yet so attached to it do they become, that few ever leave it. . . ."

W. A. Ferris
Life in the Rocky Mountains

*T*here cannot be a better test for knowing a worthless and bad character in this country than his wishing to become a freeman (free trapper) — it is a true sign of depravity, either in a wayward youth or backsliding old man."

Alexander Ross
Journal of David Thompson

THE VAGRANTS

Now from this high place
On Rampart Range
Look east—
Far below us

See
Other men coming,
Moving up the great river
Missouri, mud-rich in spring,
Sunlight on her brown and roiling
Water, stumps gouging the sand
As they roll in the current,
The men hauling from shore,
Heavy line chafing,
Heavy shoulders straining,
The river
Flowing under all
Offering herself
A road, not cheap or easy
Leading us all
Into the future,
        "The good or evil it had in store
        an experiment,"
Wrote Clark.

                We have been ourselves
                Three million years,
                Searching for ourselves
                Every instant,
                And yet we do not know
                This wilderness still
                Inside our spirit,
                The country opening
                But unknown to us
                As we are to ourselves.

Down there the descendants of Zeus
And of the Word move west
In the prairie light
Incandescent and glowing in the late afternoon
As from the center of the world.

Lewis and Clark at their head
The best we have to offer this river,

All our art and science leading us
Like a river, swelling into the west,
And after them the Mountain Men, camped now
Down on the Powder, the Big Horn,
Right at home on Rocky Fork, Clark Fork,
Rosebud and Stillwater,
All the tributaries of the Yellowstone
Swirling past our vision
On the high plain
Below this front slope . . .

They were all here—
Jim Bridger, camped on Rocky Fork
Waiting for Osborne Russell,
Joe Meek. Hugh Glass was here,
Out a ways, on the forks of the Big Horn,
Scarred and alone in winter
Hunting Fitz and Bridger, the comrades
Who had betrayed him and left him for dead.
Even Carson was here, would lose his horse
On the Three Forks trying to save a friend,
Had to double up to make it back to camp.
And old Boone! Daniel himself
Up from Missouri in 1818
Trapping the Yellowstone,
Old and alone in the West.

And those most honored
By other men. Plenty-Coups
Was home here, The-Wolf, No-Shinbone,
Gray-Bull, Medicine-Crow,
Bell-Rock, who exceeded all the others
On every count, all the men
Who knew the old way.

And names more bitter and fierce
Will come, be coming
Up this river
Till one day we rise with shackles,
Dam it, as though to hell,
Take her water for other men
Or crops or commerce,
Her body drooping, thin
As a cow, birth-fatigued
And drained by calves.

But for now
See her as road
Bending west into my heart,
Leading us into a wilderness of conflict,
The men of Troy and Rome and
The high plains hunters on horseback
From Sandia and Eden Valley . . .

Remember this time, this place
For I am Earth:
This river, these plains and hills
My body,
Have borne this coming
Scarcely to be borne . . .

LEWIS AND CLARK

April 7th, 1805 (Lewis)
"We were now about to penetrate a country at least two thousand miles
    in width, on which the foot of civilized man had never trod. The
    good or evil it had in store for us was experiment yet to
    determine. . . . However, the picture which now presented itself to me
    was a most pleasing one. I could but esteem this moment of my
    departure as among the most happy of my life."

April 15, 1805 (Lewis)
. . . I passed through the bottoms
On the starboard side.
They were partially covered with timber,
Were extensive, level, and beautiful . . .
In my walk, which was about six miles,
I heard frogs for the first time this season.
Saw greater quantities of geese feeding,
Of which I shot one,
Saw some deer and elk
But they were remarkably shy.
Also met with great numbers
Of grouse or prairie hens.
The male drums his wings
Something like a pheasant
But by no means as loud.

April 22nd, 1805 (Lewis)
Walking on the shore this evening
I met with a buffalo calf

Which attached itself to me
And continued to follow close at my heels
Until I embarked. . . .

THE MOUTH OF THE YELLOWSTONE

April 26th, 1805 (Lewis)
. . . This morning I dispatched Joseph Field
Up the Yellowstone River with orders
To examine it as far as he could . . .
He went up eight miles and in the evening returned.

He reported it to be crooked, meandering
From side to side in a broad valley,
The current gentle,
Its bed much interrupted
And broken by sandbars . . .
At five miles
He passed a large island well covered
With timber.
Three miles higher
A large creek falls in on S.E. side
Above a high bluff in which are
Several strata of coal.
The bed of the Yellowstone River
Is entirely composed of sand and mud
Not a stone of any kind
To be seen in it near its entrance.

The Indians inform
The Yellowstone is navigable
For piroques and canoes
Nearly to its source in the Rockies . . .

July 13th, 1805 (Lewis)
We eat an immensity of meat.
It requires four deer
An elk and deer
Or one buffalo
To supply us 24 hours.
Meat now forms our food principally
As we reserve our corn and flour
As much as possible for the Rocky Mountains
Which we are shortly to enter
And where, the Indians say,
Game is not very abundant.

THE THREE FORKS

July 20th, 1805 (Clark)
. . . The mosquitos very troublesome,
My man York nearly tired out.
Bottoms of my feet blistered.
Camped on the river, the feet of the men
So stuck with prickly pear
And cut with stones
They scarcely able to march
At slow gait this afternoon.

July 22nd, 1805 (Lewis)
The Indian woman assures us
The Three Forks
Are no great distance.
This piece of information cheers us
And we now console ourselves
With anticipation of shortly seeing
The head of the Missouri
Yet unknown to the civilized world.

July 24th, 1805 (Lewis)
The mountains still continue high
And seem to rise like an amphitheatre
One range above another
Until the most distant and lofty
Have their tops covered with snow.

I fear everyday
We will meet with some considerable falls
Or obstruction . . . we daily pass a great
Number of small rapids.

July 25th, 1805 (Clark)
A fine morning!
We proceeded on a few miles
To the Three Forks of the Missouri.
They are nearly of a size.
North Fork appears to have the most water,
Middle Fork is quite as large—
About 90 yards wide—
The South Fork is about 70 yards.

The bottoms are extensive and tolerable land
Covered with tall grass and prickly pear.

The hills and mountains
Are high, steep, and rocky;
The river very much divided by islands.

July 27th, 1805 (Lewis)
Ascended S.W. fork.
Believe this to be an essential point
In the geography of this western land.

We begin to feel considerable anxiety
With respect to the Snake Indians.
If we do not find them soon
Or some other nation who have horses
I fear the outcome of our voyage . . .

THE RETURN

July 11th, 1806 (Lewis)
It is now the season
When buffalo copulate
And the bulls keep a tremendous roaring.
We can hear them for many miles.
There are such numbers
That there is one continual roar
And our horses are much alarmed.

July 27th, 1806 (Lewis)
This morning at daylight
The Indians get up and crowd
Around the fire. J. Fields
Had carelessly laid his gun down.
One of the Indians—
The fellow to whom
I had given a medal last evening—
Slips behind Fields
And takes his gun and that of his brother
And is not perceived by either.
At the same instant
Two others advance
And seize the guns of Drouilliard
And myself.

J. Fields, seeing this,
Turns about to look for his gun
And sees the fellow just running off

With'er and with his brother's as well.
He calls to his brother
Who jumps up and pursues.
They overtake him about 60 paces
From the camp, seize their guns
And wrestle for them.

R. Fields stabs the Indian
To the heart with his knife.
The fellow runs about 15 steps
And falls dead. Both Fields then
Run back to camp.

Of all this I did not know
Till later.

Drouilliard, who is now awake,
Sees the Indian take hold of his gun,
Jumps up and grabs her,
But the Indian keeps his shot pouch
And D. cries, "Damn you, let go my gun!"

This wakens me
And I quickly learn the matters
When I see D. in the scuffle.
I reach for my gun but it's gone.
I draw my pistol,
Turn myself about,
And see the Indian making off.
I run at him with my pistol
And bid him lay my gun down.
He is just in the act of doing that
When the Fields return
And throw up their guns to shoot him.

I forbid it
As he does not appear to be bent
To commit any offensive act.
He drops the gun and walks slowly off.
I pick her up instantly.
Drouilliard now has his gun and pouch back
And asks me if he might kill the fellow
Which I also forbid
As the Indian does not appear
To wish to kill us.

As soon as they find us
In possession of our weapons
The Indians run
Trying to drive off all our horses.

I yell
And tell the men to fire
If they make an attempt on the horses.
Accordingly
They pursue the party
Driving the horses up the river.

I pursue the man who took my gun
Who, with another, was driving off
Part of the horses which were
To the left of camp.
I pursue so closely
They can not take twelve
Of their own horses
But continue to drive one of mine
With some others.
At a distance of 300 paces
They enter a steep niche
In the bluff with the horses before them.
I am winded
And can pursue no further.
I call to them
As I had done before
That I will shoot them
If they do not give me my horse.
I raise my gun.
One jumps behind a large rock
And calls to the other
Who turns around and stops
At a distance of 30 steps from me.

I shoot him through the belly.
He falls to his knees
And then onto his right elbow.
From this position
He raises himself, fires at me
And then crawls behind a rock.
He overshoots me.

Being bareheaded, I feel

The wind of his bullet
Most distinctly.

Not having my shot pouch
I can not reload my piece.
As there are two of them
Behind good shelters
I do not think it prudent
To rush on them with my pistol
Which I had discharged.
I therefore return leisurely
Toward camp.

We take their horses
Burn their bows and arrows,
Their shields and quivers.
I also take the flag
I gave them yesterday
But leave the medal
Around the neck of the dead man
That they might be informed
Of who we are.

The Fields return
With three of our horses.
They tell me three Indians
Swam the river—
One of them on my horse.
Two others ascended the hill
And escaped with some of the horses,
Two I had pursued into the niche.
One lay dead near the camp,
The other we cannot account for.

My Indian horse carried me
Very well—in short
Much better than my own
And leaves me
With but little reason
To complain of the robbery.

July 25th, 1806 (Clark)
. . . .at 4 P.M. arrived
At a remarkable rock
Situated in an extensive bottom.

This rock
Which I shall call Pompey's Tower
Is 200 feet high and 400 paces
In circumference
And only accessible on one side
Which is from the N.E.
The other parts being perpendicular.
On top there is tolerable soil
five or six feet thick
Covered with grass.
Indians have made two piles of stones
On top of this tower
And have engraved
On the face of this rock
The figures of animals
And near which
I have marked my name
And the day of the month and the year.

OSBORNE RUSSELL DISCOURSES
ON THE LIFE OF A TRAPPER
1837

"Here we had plenty
of wood water meat
and dry grass to sleep on,
and taking everything into consideration
we thought ourselves comfortably suited—
comfortably I say for mountaineers
not for those who never repose
on anything but a bed of down
or sit or recline on anything harder than Silken
cushions, for such would spurn at the idea
of a Hunter's talking about comfort and happiness
but experience is the best Teacher
hunger good sauce
and I really think to be acquainted with misery
contributes to the enjoyment of happiness
and to know ones self
greatly facilitates the Knowledge of Mankind—
One thing I often console myself with
and that is that the earth will lie as hard
upon the Monarch as it will on a Hunter

and I have no assurance
that it will lie upon me at all,
my bones may in a few years
or perhaps days
be bleaching on the plains in these regions
like many of my occupation
without a friend to turn even a turf upon them
after a hungry wolf has finished his feast."

JOHN COLTER

Came back
Walking up the country,
Solitary man
Even in company,

Moving south from the Yellowstone
Through the Dryhead where the buffalo
Fell to the Indian hunters,
Under the Pryor rims where the Crows
Buried their dead,
Up the Wind into that majestic
Mystery, into the Park, walking out
The high country winter
Along mammoth hot springs
And geysers.

Before Bridger
He saw everything,
Clear as sunlight on obsidian.

Saw the arrows bloom
Suddenly from the chest
Of his partner, Potts;
Was stripped,
Slapped in the face
With his partner's lungs,
Blackfeet warriors running him
Naked and barefoot through the cactus,
Seven miles to the river, running
Like a crippled antelope,
Breath and pain the same
In his lungs; his feet
A red agony of flame, running
As though separate from himself,

From his body, his body
Afloat and drifting . . .

Then diving into the river
Under the log jam
Chest swelling and sagging, cold
Water numbing the feet at last,
The only sound then, the river
And the men hunting him along the bank
Until the chest grew still, the head clear,
The rest silence and the river ringing.

Then
Walking again, alone
And naked on the land
One man alone forever
As all men are alone forever
In this life, in this immense
Place, his shadow etched
In the shadow of Pryor Mountain,
The Tetons, leaping the deadfall
In the canyon under Sunlight Basin,
Leading us forever in our desire
To people far places
As though far places abhorred emptiness
As air abhores its absence anywhere. . . .

OSBORNE RUSSELL TRAPS
THE CLARK FORK AND ROCKY FORK

We stopped and set out
Traps on the small branches
Of the Rosebud till the 11th of Octr.
Then travelled to Rocky Fork
And up it into the mountain
And encamped.

The 13th Myself and Allen
Left our companions to hunt
Mr. Fontanell's party.
We travelled down Rocky Fork
All day. There were buffalo
All across the valley
And on the benches east and west.

We reached the mouth
And camped after dark.

Next morning we went on
To "Howell's encampment,"
But our friends had left no mark
Nor had animals or enemies
Disturbed the earth since we had
Closed it upon the unfortunate Howell.
We sat down to consider.

Although the Indian Summer sun
Was warm upon us, we knew Winter
Was not long in joining us
And we could not linger
In this country where parties
Of Blackfeet ranged in every season.

I wrote a note,
Enclosed it in a buffalo horn,
Buried it at the foot of a tree
And marked the tree with a hatchet
Then mounted our Mules
And started back to the mountain.

About six miles up and hungry
We stopped to kill a cow.
As we were lying about 60 paces
From this band, Allen
Made an observation
Which I shall never forget.
Said he:
          "I have been watching these cows
          some time and I can see but one
          that is poor enough to kill.
          For,"
He said,
          "it is a shame to kill one
          of those fat Cows
          merely for two men's suppers."

So saying, he levelled
On the poorest of the lot
And brought her down.

Very late and in the dark
We stumbled on a sudden

Into an immense band of Buffalo
Who caught our scent.
They rose around us as from
The center of the earth and ran
Helter skelter in every direction
Some rushing within ten feet of us
Who did not dare to retreat
Or advance till this storm of
Wild brutes rolled away with a noise
Like an incoming tide.
We hurried on after their passing
But only a few hundred paces
Then stopped for the night
Rather than risk our limbs or lives
Among "such whirlwinds of beef."

* * * * *

After our move
To the junction with Clark's Fork
Just three miles above the Yellowstone
Two men was lookin for places to set
When a party of 60 Blackfeet
Beset them and they went into the river.
One was shot through while swimming his horse
Across, and he died. About 20 Whites
And Delawares set out to fight. They found
The Blackfeet and dove 'em onto an island
And fought 'em till it was too dark to shoot.

We lost the Nez Percey Indian
And had one White slightly wounded.
Late that night the Blackfeet mysteriously
Withdrew from the island, taking their wounded
With them, and hiding their dead.

* * * * *

19th . . . and travelled to Rocky Fork
Near the mountain. Distance was 25 mls,
Course S.W. All seven in the party
Kept together and set on Rocky Fork
Near the mountain.

On the 24th a party of Crow Indians
Approached us on their way to the Blackfoot
Village to steal horses. They had 49

Warriors and staid with us two nights
And then went to the main Camp
Which had moved onto this stream
About 20 mls down.

28th. 110 warriors came to see us
And we went with them down to the Camp
About ten mls below our own. They remained
Throughout the next day and then left
For the Blackfeet camped on the Three Forks.

* * * * *

30th. We began again to follow my intent
To set on Rocky Fork. . . . As we travelled
It began to rain and we stopped
Not by rain but to approach a band
Of Buffaloe and Myself and one Comrade
(A Canadian) were crouching along near
Some bushes. We roused a large
Grizzly Bear who sprang upon the Canadian
Who had been in front five or six feet.

He put one forepaw upon my companion's head,
The other he placed on his left shoulder
Then pushed him one side about 12 feet
As if my partner had been a cat,
The bear still keeping his course as tho.
Nothing had been in his path.

We soon found the fright exceeded the wound.
My friend received no injury from the encounter
Except to his coat which was badly torn.

Next day travelled up Rocky Fork,
Then left the stream at right Angles,
Heading in a westerly direction
And walked parallel to the mountains
About ten mls and set on the stream we call
Bodair's Fork and then downstream and camped.

TRAPPING PRYOR CREEK:
OSBORNE RUSSELL RECOLLECTS
MAJOR MEEK AND DAVE CROW

Major Meek, Joe Meek
Tall Virginian
Twelve years in the mountains
Riding a white Indian pony.
Mountain Man.

When asked what was the news
He said,

      "News! Well I have been—
      me and Dave here—
      over on Pryor's Fork to set our traps.

      "Found old Ben Johnson's boys there
      just walkin up and down them air streams
      with they hands on air hips
      gathering plums.

      "Gabe, you know where the Pryor
      leaves the cut bluffs goin up to it?
      Tough country there,
      steeper'n a cow's face.
      Well after you get out the hills
      on the right hand fork
      there is scrubby box elders
      'bout three miles along the creek
      up to where a little spring puts in
      from the right? They's lots a plum trees
      round the mouth of it
      an some old beaver dams
      on the main creek?

      "Well sir, we went up there and set
      yesterday morning; I set two traps
      right below the mouth of that little branch
      and in them old dams.
      Dave set his down the creek apiece.

      "After we got done we cruised around some.
      Best plums I ever see is there,
      trees'r loaded and breaking down.
      Finest kinda plums—

large as pheasants eggs and sweet as sugar.
No wonder them rascally savages
like that place so well.

"Well sir, after we had eat
me and Dave took down the creek
and staid the night on a little branch
in the hills there.
This morning we started to our traps—
Dave's first—
and there's a four year old 'spade' in one,
one had a foot only,
and the rest was undisturbed.
So we went on to mine to the mouth of the branch.
I rode on five or six steps ahead of Dave and
just as I got opposite the first trap
I heard a rustlin in the bushes.
I looked around
and pop pop pop went the guns
covering me with smoke so close
I could see the blanket wads
coming out the muzzles.

"Well sir, I wheeled old Too Shebit here
and a ball struck her in the neck,
just touched the bone
and we pitched heels over head
but Too Shebit raised a runnin
and I on her back,
the savages just squattin and grabbin at me.
But I raised a fog for about half a mile
and caught up with Dave
and here we be."

HUGH GLASS

Never got here
First trip.
Not this high up the country.
What happened to him
Happened on the Grand.

The story got around—
Not much of who he was,
But what he did got told
Over and over.

Not around any campfire
Near Bridger, of course,
But plenty others.

You can imagine the exaggeration—
The white bear's size,
All the details mind could paint
Of mauling, the reward offered any
Who would wait until he died.
The theft and betrayal—
It all got told
Winter nights around the fires,
And the arguments:
How he made it, what kept him
Alive, aside from hatred and desire,
Hope of revenge on those who took
The one thing most precious—
His gun.

Second time
Glass came to this country
Walking up the Yellowstone,
The cold winter wind
Whipping the loneliness into Indians
Into giants, into Bears
Waiting along the river bank
Under the brush and snow,
Then walking the forks of the Big Horn
To face young Bridger
Finding all the anger burned away
By wind and age and walking—
Just pity and disgust finding Jim
Who was only nineteen;
The meeting leaving him
"Old Gabe," a man,
Honest at last and forever
After that facedown with the truth.

Heading back down the river
Tracking old Fitz who survived
Only because an army Captain
Was not about to see
One of his men shot by anyone
Not a redskin—
No matter how just the shot
Might be.

So the Captain got Glass's gun
Back to Glass
And Fitz kept his blood
Inside his veins
And Hugh took off again
For the Southwest
Alone
As Colter was alone
Walking down the front slope
To Santa Fe
To begin again.

HARVEY'S AWFUL DEED

Larpenteur had a friend,
Harvey,
Who always kept a No. 1 horse,
And soon overtook the Indian
Who had shot their cow.
When he got within a few steps
Fired
And broke the Indian's thigh.
The Indian fell off his horse
And there he lay.

Harvey came up
Got off his horse,
Took his seat near the wounded man
And said,
        "Now comrade
        I have got you.
        You must die,
        But before you die,
        you must smoke a pipe with me."

He lit his pipe
And made the poor man smoke.
Then said,
        "I am going to kill you,
        but I will give you a little time
        to look over your country."

The Indian replied,
        "I was a fool; I killed your cow.
        But now you have broken my thigh.

This ought to make us even.
Spare my life."

"No-o-o,"
Said Harvey,
        "Look well,
        for the last time,
        at those hills —
        at all those paths which lead to
        the fort, where you came
        with your parents to trade,
        and where you played with your sweethearts —
        look at that, will you,
        for the last time."

So saying
With his gun pointed at the head
Of his victim, he pulled the trigger
And the Indian was no more.

WHAT TO DO
IF YOU MEET A BEAR

A Greenhorn approached
Two old-timers:

        "What do I do
        if I meet a bear?"
He asked.

T. A. Anderson said,
        "Spit in his eye."

To which Sam Hill responded,
        "Most of us don't spit too good
        over our shoulder."

ZENAS LEONARD
ON GRIZZLIES

The Grizzly Bear
is very numerous in these parts
and the most ferocious animal
to inhabit these prairies.
They no sooner see you
but make at you with open mouth.

If you stand still
they come within two or three yards,
stand upon their hind feet
and look you in the face.

If you have fortitude
enough to face them
they will turn and run off
but if *you* turn
they will most assuredly
tear you to pieces;
strong proof of the fact
no wild beast however
daring and ferocious
unless wounded
will attack the face of man.

ZENAS RECOUNTS
A GRIZZLY TALE

Two members of our party
unexpectedly came upon
five grizzly bears
sleeping in the grass —
two old ones
and three cubs.
The old ones made for the hunters
with open mouth.

One of the men
was an old practitioner
in such matters,
the other was set to run.
The former stood quite composed
and urged his comrade
to stand his ground as well.

Having a good gun
carrying a one ounce ball
which he called
        "Knock him stiff,"
when the bear
came within reach
he discharged his gun
in her mouth,
which treatment, he said,
        "Gave her a very bad cough."

The other hunter
being inspired with courage
killed the second adult
in a similar manner
and since the cubs seemed
indisposed to leave
they killed them also.

This day's hunt, says Zenas
Was exceedingly lucky
for all.

RENDEZVOUS

I

A principal task at rendezvous
Was to drink, and all agreed
Joe was known to drink a mite
And maybe more —

Camped on Horse Creek, summer of '33
He did over-indulge considerable.
And they's a mad wolf comes
Prowling around camp. Now
This wolf hangs around several nights
And nobody's sleepin too deep
'Cept Joe Meek whose heart is big
And belly full of whiskey.

An one night this wolf
Bites old Holmes, tears his ear near off,
Bites three men on the face,
And tries a nip from others too.
They's a hellacious hooraw.

All the shouting and shooting of rifles
Fails to wake old Meek.

Next day Stuart tells him,
        "You was so drunk
        that wolf coulda bit you easy."

        "Yes,"
Joe says,
        "An it woulda killed him sure —
        or else cured him!"

JIM BRIDGER

Out on the prairie alone
Jim got jumped by Blackfeet
Who shot his horse before
He could snap a cap,
Vestal says.

The horse reared and bucked
As the arrows struck
And Bridger dropped his gun.

A warrior snatched it up
But Bridger got himself some luck
And his wounded animal took him safe
Back to his own camp.

Next day, as usual,
He went around the camp
Inspecting weapons.
Irish Maloney's rifle was a mess.

> "What would you expect
> to do with that
> if the Blackfeet charged
> right now?"
Demanded Jim.

> "Begorra,"
Said Maloney,
> "I would throw it to 'em and run—
> the way you did!"

A greenhorn one day asked,
> "How long you been out here, Jim?"

> "See that hill?
> When I first see the mountains
> that hill was only a hole in the ground."

RENDEZVOUS

II

Passing around the kettle
Filled with whiskey,
> "One of the party,"
Meeks recounts,

"poured the contents over the head
of a tall red-headed fellow.
Can't remember his name,"
Says Meek,
"but as he poured, this fella
was reciting the baptismal rite."

Another friend
With a brand from the fire
Touched the redhead ablaze.

When some of the company
Perceived the danger
They beat him with pack-saddles
To smother the flames.

"Between the burning
and the beating,"
Says Joe,
"the poor wretch
nearly lost his life
and never fully recovered."

JOE MEEK GETS CAPTURED
BY THE CROWS

I was trapping on Rocky Fork
Joe says
Been out about five days
Solitary and by myself
Till the Crows come.

They had the prairie;
I was forced to run
For the creek bottom.
But the beaver had turned
The creek to mire with their dams,
An while I was struggling
With my mule in the marsh
The Indians came after me
With tremendous yells,
Firing a random shot or two
As they closed.

I knew it was death this time—
Unless Providence interfered

To save me—and I didn't think
Providence would do it.

The head chief
When he saw the looks of *Sally*
Called out to me to put her down
And I should live.

Well I like to live—
Being then in the prime of life—
An though it hurt me powerful
I resolved to part with Sally
An laid her down.

The chief picked her up
An they led me
To the high plain south
Of the Fork.

Now
That is nice country, but—
I'd rather been
Most anyplace else!

LIVER-EATING JOHNSON

Well, yes,
Harry Field said,
I knew him
When he was night
Marshall in Red Lodge.
Quiet, self-possessed sort,
Not much given
To empty talk or idle chatter.
Kids liked him.
But he wasn't one
You could just talk to
Real easy. Always tried
To be careful,
Not wanting to cause any
Affront you know.
However, I did finally
Ask him if he really ate
The liver of all those Crows
Like everybody said.

Well, no,
John Johnson said,
I never did.
What happened was
A couple of dudes
Was out here
Wanting me and Del
To take 'em hunting.
But we didn't like to do that.
Even the Crows
Was being ugly them days
An those two
Sure didn't appear to be any help
If there was trouble.
And we wasn't anxious
To court trouble
Just so's they could have some
Sport. But they allowed
As how that was just
The kind of excitement
They was looking for
An how they was considerable
Tough enough to hold their own . . .
An they got around Del
Somehow, and he always could
Find his way around me,
So we found ourselves
Hunting, south of the Yellowstone
Below where Laurel is now.
An sure enough
We ran into some Crows
All turned out in paint
And finery and bent
On our demise.
Well Del and me had our hands
Full, while these two
Dogs just lay in the dirt
And whined and never
Snapped a cap to help.
We was both disgusted
An I thot to show them
A thing or two
About how serious this country
Really is.

So I stepped over
One of the dead Crow
Warriors, slit his belly open,
Cut out the liver,
Held it high, tipped my head up
And opened my mouth
As though to gulp it down.
I had my back to those fellas
But they thought I was
Really eatin it
An both turned sick.
While they was bent
Over their most recent
Meal, I just dropped that liver
An kicked it off under the sage.
Del always was windy
An willin to help.
He told 'em it was
Routine, and it all got
Blowed up from there,

Harry said,
John Johnson said.

HUNGER

John Macdonnell was talking
About food,
          "Here I saw the first dog
          (a large Black Indian one
          that Auge the interpreter
          killed in Lac Croche) eaten,"
He says,
          "He castorated him as soon as he fell
          to prevent the rank taste in the flesh.
          The hair of the animal was singed off
          as Canadians singe their hogs
          and then washed clean in water."
But nearly everybody had tried dog
And deemed it better'n crow.
Ross Cox had his story:
          "As our provisions were nearly consumed
          we were obliged to purchase twenty dogs.
          It was the first time I had eaten

on the flesh of this animal,
and nothing but stern necessity
could have induced me to partake of it.
The president of our mess
called it mutton
which it somewhat resembles in taste.
We generally had it roasted,
but the Canadians preferred it boiled,
and the majority of them seem to think it
superior to horse-flesh. In this, however,
I entirely differ from them."

Old Larpenteur knew short rations
When he had them
And recognized a good meal when he ate it:
"The day we moved in was a great holiday
and in the evening a great feast was given us.
It consisted of half a pint of flour to each man;
one cup of coffee, one of sugar,
and one of molasses, to four men.
Out of this was made,"
Larpenteur said,
"a becoming feast
consisting of thick pancakes, the batter
containing no other ingredients
than pure Missouri water, greased with buffalo
tallow; but as I had had nothing of the kind
for upward of six months, I thought I had
never tasted anything so good in my life,
and swore I would have plenty of the like
if I ever got back to the States."

THE SAYINGS OF JOE MEEK

I

Roast punkin's not so bad,
I've eat worse in the mountains.
Roast punkin is buffalo tongue
compared to ants
or moccasin soles.

II

I said to myself
Joe Meek you have always been

and Joe Meek you shall remain,
Go ahead, Joe Meek!

III

(On meeting a Blackfeet war party)

Running away from them
will not increase their numbers
and might help me defend myself.

IV

(On war)

Well, war always was
a poor makeout.
You might save your skin
but where's your mule?

V

(After charging a band of Indians singlehanded)

I took their compliments (his friends')
quite naturally. I reckoned it wasn't worthwhile
to tell them I couldn't hold my horse.

VI

(Teaching his son to speak his first words)

Say, "Goddamn you!"

VII

(Sampling the beef in a city restaurant)

That'll do.
Fetch me four pounds of the same.

VIII

Live and let live—
But if it comes to one or the other
I'd rather live.

V. WEST OF THE MISSOURI

*T*he descent on the west side was so abrupt
that we were compelled to let our wagons
down in part by attaching ropes and letting the
men hold on behind. . . ." (From Absaroka
Ridge)

     James A. Pritchard
     The Overland Diary

*B*ook A commences my diary September 11,
1863. Read the year out and turn back to
January first and read for the year 1864 in this
book down to September 11, 1864. Then com-
mence in Book B at September 11 and read the
year out."

     A. G. Noble
     Diary of A. G. Noble

WEST OF THE MISSOURI

Now
Behind the fur men
Look again
Below us to the east,
See the white tops of wagons
Bulge and sway above the horizon
Crawling onto the prairie where
Walter Pigman says,
        "The most interesting
        and romantic scenery
        is presented to the beholder;
        one unbounded plain
        of high rolling ground
        looking more like a beautiful farm
        stretching itself before one
        without a tree to rest the eye upon,
        forcibly reminding you
        of the wave of the troubled ocean . . .
        The track of the emigrants' train
        was all that was to be seen."

The train
A great pale slug
Crawling across my flat belly,
        "For miles,"
Says Delano,
        "to the extent of vision
        an animated mass of being
        always in our view.
        Long trains of wagons,
        their white canvas covers moving slowly,
        a multitude of horsemen, prancing,
        companies of men on foot . . .

        "The scene was not a gorgeous one,
        yet the display of banners
        from many wagons,
        the multitude of armed men,
        all looked as if a mighty army
        were on the march.

                'Lone Star'
        would be seen rising
        over a hill.

'Live Hoosier'
rolled along

'Wild Yankee'

'Rough and Ready'

'Enterprise'

'The Dawdle Family'

were all moving
at a slow and steady pace
with a right smart sprinkle
of names following
at intervals.
'Elephant'

'Buffalo'

'Gold Hunters!'

painted on the canvas
of the wagons. . . ."

Fifty thousand persons in an endless
Train, says Hulbert,
Travelers and fellow travelers
Rarely out of sight
Of one another,
"The ratio being 16 men
to one woman and three women
to every child."

And trudging with them
36,000 oxen, 18,000 horses,
7000 mules and milch cows,
And 2000 sheep,

All bent on crossing
My lively prairie,
Leaving their scars
Like stretch marks on my belly,
Cutting a swath through buffalo
And elk, all the fair game;
Cutting me open at last
For gold or grain,
The people streaming
Into this new land,
Recreating the life

They thought they had left behind,
Destroying whatever lay before;
Grass and game gone
After the first few miles
Of wagons; hard times
Left in the schooners' wake
For those who came behind . . .
And for me. . . .

THE TRACK

Old Archy Hulbert reports,
As a rule
we are all overloaded,
and no matter what condition mules,
horses or oxen are in,
heavy wagons mired to the hubs
make a problem—
for their owners
and for everybody behind them.

No one wants to drive
into wheel tracks a foot and a half
deep. So it's try to get around,
taking in new ground
and maybe bogging down
worse than your neighbor.

So our "trail" is rods wide.
If it wasn't that wide
it might be that deep.

Except at intervals
hundreds of miles apart
no one track can or does
take care of the traffic,
and our trail usually
consists of three or four
parallel roadways or
six or eight wheel-tracks
as the case may be.

At coulee or river crossings
Our tracks may multiply
into twenty

as new fording places are opened
when old ones get "rotten."

If I am any judge
unless they are all as strong
as Uncle Bob's palatial chariot
two thirds of them will never see
California.

THE TRAIL

Pritchard's Account

Wednesday, June 13th, 1849
At 3 P.M.
we struck a dry branch
and passing down it some distance
we came to a spring and Pool
of water strongly impregnated
with Sulpher & Alkali.
We there watered ourselves
& Animals
and continued till 7
when we struck a small branch
that afforded a scanty supply
that was impregnated
with the Carbonet of Soda & Alkali.

We could barely use it
for coffee.

The grass was tolerable
but we had to keep a guard
with the mules all the time
to keep them from swamping
in the spouty places.
A man would sink
to his neck instantly.
Several of the men fell in
during the night.
I saw five head of Oxen
sunk down to their hornes.
Distance today
30 miles.

Thursday, June 14th, 1849
At 4 P.M.
we were on the road
endeavoring to get away
from the unpleasant and dangerous place.

During the night
3 of the mules belonging to Basye's train
fell into the Quagmire.

The men of an Ox train
spent the morning digging and hauling out
their cattle.
Some 7 or 8 of them had sunk down
head hornes and all.
We enjoyed several hearty laughs
at the boys to see them walk
right into the Soda
up to their eyes
without the formality of
knocking at the door.

PIGMAN'S JOURNAL

The Sun

May 11, 1850
At noon it will appear
as though we were coming
on to a lake
having the appearance
of being on fire
and the horsemen in front look
as if they were traveling
on this fiery lake,
also the teams look
to be gliding upon the surface
enveloped in flame.
The same frequently appears
in our rear.

Wind, Dust, Rain, Snow

May 1, 1850
After morning we started
but were driven into camp

or be torn to pieces.
Sought shelter in a deep ravine.
Several teams in the company —
how they subsist on this poor grass
is a mystery to me,
but they make from fifteen
to twenty miles a day.

Often the dust blinds our teams
and we have to stand
and hold them at night,
or the wind blows the tents down
and rain drenches everything.
The wind today is bitter cold
from the north.

May 26, 1850
Camped in a recess
in Independence Rock.
The rock is a great
curiosity, it stands alone
in the Sweet Water Valley
and is 150 feet high,
its base covering more
than 25 acres of ground.
There are thousands of names
engraved on its sides.
I visited its summit;
it was a dreary sight
with everything covered with snow.

Here the packers had
a hard time, having to stand
all night in the recesses
of this rock with cold wind
and snow beating on them
with no shelter but the rock.

BUFFALO

I

Delano's Diary

May 31
Saw buffaloes for the first time

in considerable numbers
on the opposite side of the fork,
and were much amused in seeing
the emigrants dashing in upon them
in gallant style.

One was shot in our sight.
Not only was the chase exciting
but witnessing it was extremely so
and as the herd dashed off
we could scarcely repress a desire
to be after them ourselves.

II

Pigman's Journal

May 8
The boys killed a buffalo
and I cooked the supper
sitting upon a buffalo's head,
cooking buffalo on a fire
made of buffalo chips.

III

Miller's Tale

September 12
As we were hitching up this morning
we discovered a couple of buffaloe.
Saddling Frank I started after them.

After an exciting chase of half an hour
I finished one of them
putting a ball through his heart.

Four of us on horseback
chased him among the bluffs
where he finally expired.
After tremendous exertions
with a dull knife
I severed a ham
and after some time
arrived in camp with it.
Very much elated.

IV

Pritchard's Account

Just as we were leaving
a Buffalo Bull was chased
into camp.
A great excitement
was instantly created.
Every man sprang to his gun,
and each took a shot
at the Old Gentlman
as he passed.
Not one shot seemed to take effect
or turn his course.

I caught my Gun
after I saw that he
was still on his feet,
mounted a horse and was about
overtaking him
when he pitched into the River.
I, however, dismounted
and took a deliberate fire at him
as he swam off. The ball
took effect and sank him down,
but he rose and made shore
and finally made his escape
as we had no means of crossing
after him.

GRASS

Pigman's Journal

May 1
We are now 200 miles
from the Missouri River
and see some signs of grass.

May 2
No grass yet.
Our feed begins to fail.

May 5
Early on we started to hunt for grass.
Dennison's train is a few days

ahead of us, burning the grass
at every camping.

May 8
Have traveled fifteen miles
but find no grass.

May 12
Today we would like to lay up
but a majority believe
we ought to travel on,
the grass not being up sufficiently.

CHOLERA

Delano's Diary

About four o'clock on Monday morning
we were awakened by groans and cries
of distress. We sprang out and found
poor Harris, writhing and agonized
with cholera. I gave him a large dose
of laudanum, the only palliative we had,
and sent for a physician who came
within the hour. For about three hours
Harris suffered intense pain, vomiting,
purging, cramps and cold extremities while
a clammy sweat started from every pore. We had
to move him to a more quiet and secluded spot.
The evacuations and vomiting ceased,
his limbs became warm, his eye brightened.
He thought, as we did, that he was better.

He remained in this state about three hours
during which time we continued our exertions,
rubbing him, and making the applications as
advised by the physician, when all looked
upon him as out of danger. Suddenly
and without warning, he began to gasp and
in five minutes a corpse lay before us.
We could scarcely credit our senses . . .
We laid him out on the ground, decently,
and as well as slender means would allow,
and Brown and myself lay near him that night,
keeping a melancholy watch over the remains
of our companion and friend . . .

We dug his grave ourselves
in the morning
and with no tolling bell
to mark the sad requiem,
we buried him
in a cluster of trees,
by the side of a rivulet.

INDIANS!

I

Pigman's Journal

April 26
There are signs of Indians here
but none to be seen.
This nation is 12,000 strong.
There being no grass
is the reason they are not
more numerous along the route.

May 12
Abundance of Indians to be seen.
We had some fine sport
letting them shoot at
one-half dimes and dimes
with their arrows.

May 14
At noon we were surrounded again
by the Sioux Indians
who were very friendly.
Whirlwind, their chief,
has often punished his own men
for disturbing the whites.

II

Miller's Tale

We espied about a half a mile from us
at a mail station a crowd of Indians.
Old muskets, rifles, shot guns and revolvers
were immediately invoked and put in running order
after which, unable to discover over a dozen
to our 55, we advanced.
They proved to be a party of Sioux

and pretended to be on a buffalo hunt.
After begging what they could
they left us.

We shortly came on Baker's Ranch
and a mail station,
both burned last night,
the smoke of which we saw
at our camp.

DRYSPELL

Delano's Diary

We had been toiling
five days over rugged roads
scantily supplied with grass
and good water,
feeling certain on reaching the Platte
these would be abundantly supplied.

We accordingly took an early start
so that we could reach
the destined point in good season
to lay by and rest.
The day was sultry,
yet weary as we were
we drove on with spirit,
over the hills to the valley
of the Platte.

On descending the hill
instead of good grass and promised rest
we found a barren soil
that bore only weeds
which our cattle would not eat,
and a sandy road
which doomed us to another day
of toil and disappointment.

There was no help
for it, and we were compelled
to go on all day
with the naked Black Hills
peering down on us,

like goblins laughing
at our way-worn wretchedness,
in the language of Macbeth's witches:

> "Double, double, toil and trouble,
> Fire burn and cauldron bubble."

Psaw!
If our cauldron is full
we'll upset it!

So drive on, Hazel.
Ho! for California!

VI. THE TREE

No, we are not like cut flowers that make up a bouquet: we are like the leaves and buds of a great tree . . . let life draw from yet more distant sources the sap which flows through its innumerable branches. . . ."

> Teilhard de Chardin
> *Hymn to the Universe*

The world turns and the world changes, But one thing does not change. In all my years, one thing does not change. However you disguise it, this thing does not change

> The perpetual struggle of Good and Evil."

> T. S. Eliot
> *Choruses from "The Rock"*

Where I begin is all one to me. Wherever I begin I will return again."

> Parmenides
> *fragment V*

THE TREE

A great cottonwood grows along
the bank of a small stream. Longer
than any of our old men or old women
can remember, this tree has grown
from the center of the earth. The
earth and the tree are inseparable;
each necessary to the other's richest
life.

Among all our people there is not yet
one who knows how deep the roots go,
nor yet how far they spread under the
ground.

The tree has many limbs.
In the spring the smallest tips of the
tree reveal light brown husks. Inside
each husk is a green bud. Each bud
grows from the end of a single shoot
which rises from one of many twigs.
The twigs reach out from a limb ex-
tending from the heavy trunk climbing
out from its maze of roots.

Within, the bud is a bit of green folded
tightly around itself.

When sunlight and rainfall and circumstance
are in right proportion, the bud unfolds.
It becomes a leaf, green, and in proper
time, golden.

Without water or sun, without the mysterious elements of the earth which are
drawn upward through the roots, the trunk,
the limbs, the bud draws tighter and
tighter within itself; the tiny leaf
shrivels, the bud becomes very hard
and dies.

At the death of even the poorest bud,
every leaf trembles, the great trunk
shudders, the whole earth stirs.

VII. LITANY OF
THE BUFFALO

*B*uffaloe are very particular
In their choice
Always preferring short uplands
Grass to the more lush
Growth of alluvial bottoms.

They are taught by Nature
To choose such food
As is most palatable,
And She has provided
That the most palatable
Is most nutritious
And best suited to their condition
And that condition is best calculated
To supply the necessities of her rude
Children for whom all was prepared.

Thus Nature
Looks with a smile of derision
Upon the magnified efforts of Art
To excel her works
By a continual breach of her laws."
    Osborne Russell
    Journal of a Trapper

*B*uffalo, antelopes and elk are abundant in
the vicinity and we are therefore living
well."
    John Kirk Townsend
    Narrative of a Journey

*T*is an awful sight. Such a waste
of the finest meat in the world!
Probably ten thousand buffalo have
been killed in this vicinity this
winter. . . ."
    Granville Stuart
    Pioneering in Montana

WHAT THE BUFFALO SAID

I lived on Rock Creek
Over the East Bench
Above Red Lodge
West to Red Lodge Creek
Beyond the hills where Jim Burnett
Still keeps his vestigial remnants
Of the great herds,
Past Roscoe, Absaroka, Columbus,
Above Rapelje
Where you can still see the pish-kin
On the prairie,
Over the hills at Hardin,
The pine breaks and plains
At Lame Deer,
The foothills and prairies
And through Bozeman Pass into the mountains,
Back east of the Mississippi, the Ohio,
From Canada to Mexico, my numbers
Over sixty million.

I walked lightly upon the land,
My trails now gone from sight,
Just furrows in the mind,
A memory in the Earth's unconscious.

My name is bison.
On the plains they call me
Bison bison bison
Nee Bison antiquus figginsi,
Bison Taylori, Bison latifrons
Or Bison occidentalis.

In the mountains
I am Bison bison athabascae.

You can call me buffalo—
Everyone else does,
And I've been called worse—
"Buffler," or "Buff," for short
And some have even called me
"Stupid," for I am both
Gregarious and giving;
For thousands of years
I have given myself
That others might live.

Peoples of many cultures
Have been nourished,
Housed, clothed and accoutered
With my varying parts.

Before man
I was here. Men who know
Tell me
40,000 years ago I lived
In New Jersey. The smoke
Was not too bad then,
But industry and agriculture
Became too much for me.
I left.

15,000 B.C. Folsom men
Killed 27 of my ancestors
In one place.

10,000 years ago
Men of the old way
Killed 300 more in Colorado.

We had an agreement
And I did not mind.

My skin has turned
The arrows of enemies,
Kept your thinner skins warm,
Made safe the tender soles
Of feet attacked by thorns or frost;
My raw hides surrounded
The most precious ceremonial
Icons `when en route, and painted,
Kept the records straight of battles
And events so grave and weighty
No man dared forget.

And when those cultures died
I gave myself to yours
For sport and entertainment.
Not an enterprise deigned ignoble
If one can count court jesters,
Boxers, ball-players,
Strippers and stand-up comedians.

When all my hides were shipped
This prairie stank with flesh and death;

You took my bones for china cups
And drank your tea from a sea
Of grass by way of me.

WHAT THE RUNNER SAID

Sure, son, I'll tell all how
It was, till lately anyhow.
But first yuh gotta understand,
Runnin buffalo is like fishin—
You have to be smarter than the fish
An you have to keep your hook in the water.
See.

Now a big male buff
Stands 6, maybe 7 feet tall,
Weighs up to 2000 pounds.
Probly averages closer to 16, 17 hunnert.
The female is smaller—
Maybe 5 foot at the shoulder,
Goes around 7 to 9 hunnert pounds.

They rut mid-July till late August,
Calves'er born in April'er May.
In the old days
I seen Blackfeet pen 'em,
Kill 'em with spears.
An I heard tell about others—
Crows, Sioux an like them—
Chasen 'em over the bluffs.
Fact, Dary says that's how this
Dry Head country got named.
Old Tip of the Fur
Went down here, found this cliff—
Where Hoodoo Creek and the Dry Head
Come together, yuh know?
He and his boys stompeded them critters
Over this cliff in a great bunch.
Ole Tip had all the heads whacked off
And stacked in one spot.
From then on
Whenever them Indians made a kill here
They always cut off the heads
An piled 'em up in the same place—
Late as 1890 they did that—

"In time there was a massive pile
of dried buffalo skulls,"
Dary says,
And that's where this country
Gets the name.

I have been hunted with fire
And survived;
Surrounded, driven over ledges
Struck by arrows, by darts
By lances and by lead
And survived.
My real dangers were
Wagons, railroads,
Fences and ploughs.

After a good hunt, Sandoz says,
Indians painted the finest robe
Fixed it all up with quills
By the finest seamstress in the tribe
Then took it up on a high hill
And left it there.
Way of sayin thanks
To the Great Powers
To Earth, Mother and Grandmother
And Sky, Father and Grandfather
And to buffalo
For all those his kind
Who died that the Indian
Might live.

We had an agreement.
There was a word between us . . .

I loved to roll in dust
Stretch, rub my head
Hard into the ground

I seen old bulls
Had halfa inch a horn
Worn off on the outside
From rooting around in the dust.

Rock on my horns
Clear over on my hump
Throw dust in great clouds
To catch the sunlight
And escape the flies.

Tough headed Buzzards!
Charley Russell used to tell
Bout a fella hitched two of 'em
To a plough. They pulled good enough
But he couldn't get 'em turned!
No neck to 'em, and their heads
Wouldn't pull to rein or rope.
Ploughed north in the spring
South in the fall;
Nice straight furrow, deep and true
One end in Canada
The other in Mexico.
'Member Joe Meek yarnin one time
Bout runnin buffalo on horses.
Risky business, he says,
> "How they do thunder along!
> They give us a pretty sharp race,
> Take care!
> Down goes a rider!
> Away goes his horse with the herd!
>
> "Do you think we stopped
> To look after the fallen man?
> Not us!
> We rather thought that was fun
> And if one got killed
> He was unlucky, that's all.
> Plenty more men!
> Couldn't bother with him!"

Sometimes a horse destroyed himself
Destroying me. Dust would blind
His eyes; a hole or rock or gully
Became a trap for slender legs . . .

> Tom McHugh told me
> Custer shot his wife's favorite
> Thoroughbred one time.
> He run old "Custis Lee" up alongside
> A good sized bull,
> Was jest set to shoot with his pistol
> When the bull lurched toward him
> And his horse veered away so quick
> To keep his seat
> He grabbed the reins with both hands
> And accidentally,

". . . *pressed the trigger*
and discharged the weapon,
the ball entering Lee's neck
near the top of his head
and penetrating his brain.
This produced instant death,"
He said, a for sure truth.
He got hisself pitched heels over head
Into the dirt.
Didn't get hurt none,
But had to write to Libby,
Trying to explain how
Her favorite nag wouldn't be available
When she came out next time.

Course horses ain't hardly strong enough
For this work anyhow. Better'n foot, mind,
And a good one'll catch a buff in half a mile.
But that's a good one, a real prize.
Frances Haines says you got one that good
You bring him inside at night
If there's danger near. Let your women
Sleep outside!

I became for some
The medium for exchange

Everybody them days used
Their meat for food,
Their hides for coin.
Swap for anything with robes.
'Member some Crows one time
Bet Jim McNaney $1200 worth of robes
They had a race horse
Could beat his saddle mare.
Naturally they lost the race
But them Red Brothers
Paid off them hides
Way you or me'd cash a draft.

My hide was tough . . .
But not enough.

Well,
Buffalo dress out about half—
Like beef or elk—

> *Big green hide can weigh*
> *150 pounds from a bull,*
> *Dry hide'll go about a third a hide*
> *Still green.*
> *Young cows'll make the best robes.*
> *Take 'em in late autumn.*
> *Their winter coats're short and thick.*
> *Scrape 'em thin and let 'em dry,*
> *Rub the hide with brains.*
> *They come out real fine!*

My own brains used
To tan my hides!

> *Army used 'em for winter gear.*
> *They're bulky but soft,*
> *An damn! They are pretty!*
> *Member the boys at Keogh*
> *Standin on the porch steps*
> *One winter, all decked out*
> *In buffalo coats so's L.A.*
> *Could get their picture.*

Men thought their guns
Were beautiful,
Handled them with care.

> *Well,*
> *If you was bent on goin*
> *You had to get a big gun when you went.*
> *They was best for that work.*
> *Ballard's, Henry's, Spencers all'd shoot*
> *Straight as you could hold 'em,*
> *But they was just a little light.*
> *Took a good 50 caliber breechloader,*
> *Either Sharps or Remington,*
> *With three inch brass either straight*
> *Or necked down—*
> *Didn't make no difference*
> *Though some picked one over the other.*
> *You'd reload at night*
> *After ever day's shootin.*
> *Fer God's sake watch the sparks!*

> *Took about 100, 110 grains of three f*
> *And a ball of lead about an ounce*

(320 grains at least, maybe 5, 550).
You had to do some shootin
To find the load just right for yer gun.
When you got it,
Cutcha off an old cartridge
The right length. It'd make a measure
To get it just the same ever time.
Good gun'd shoot straight out about
800 yards, weigh 12 to 18 pounds,
Had double sett triggers
And a twenty power scope.

Cody called his gun
"Lucretia Borgia!"

Whole shebang might set you back
A hunderd, two hunderd, maybe
Even two hunderd fifty bucks.
If you was set with a good gun
You'd be all right.

As fer the rest,
You could get by with less
But Haines says two hunters
Took a ton one time.
Now I never seen this, mind,
But he's a truthful man,
Says they took
          1600 pounds a lead
          400 pounds a powder
For just one season's hunt!
Shoot, they had more ammunition
Than all the troops at Fort Phil!

If you couldn't get
Eighty or ninety buffs
At three hunderd yards
For ever hunderd rounds
Then turn in your Sharps
An let a man shoot!

Course it wasn't cheap to get a start.
L.A. said in 1882 McNaney's took
          2 wagons
          2 four horse teams
          2 saddle horses

2 wall tents
1 cook stove
3 Sharps breechloaders
(One 45-90, one 45-70, one 45-120.
Yuh go by the numbers, see;
First number's the size of bore,
Second is how much powder yuh drop).

Plus

50 pounds of powder
550 pounds of lead
4500 primers
600 brass cases
4 sheets of patch paper
60 Wilson skinning knives
3 butcher's steles
1 portable grindstone

And for provisions
flour
coffee
sugar
an air-tights enough to last.
Set 'em back 1400 bucks at Miles.

But like L.A. says,
"Any rifleman in those days
could go out an stalk
an animal or two
and start a stampede,
but the man worthwhile
that could keep a half a dozen
Skinners at work
must know how to get
a 'stand.' "

Well, actually,
You could make a stand
By sittin
In a grove a trees
Along the side of a hill
Or on a ridge above a draw.
Main thing, you had to be methodical
An cold, plumb cold.

You'd shoot the leader first—
That was generally a cow—
You'd get so you could tell.
But you didn't shoot to kill; you'd
Try for lungs, or bust down the hips
To anchor 'em awhile.
The rest would gather round
To see what's wrong or smell the blood.
Then if one would turn away
You'd try for the neck or heart
And kill 'em clean.

When the others'd start to mill
You could drop 'em all, or most,
One by one.

When a big stand
Required fast and steady shooting
And the guns had been switched often
And the canteens were empty
Men urinated on their barrels
To cool them down.

But it ain't easy to do all that.
You have to know how to time your shots,
Gauge the wind and guess the distance
Accurate from 200 hunderd yards and more.
Then stay steady enough to kill 'em
Dead in their tracks.

Your skinners, if they was good,
Could skin out 25, maybe 30 hides a day—
More if they was rested up.
They'd stack 'em ten hides high,
Wrap 'em in green thongs
Or roll 'em flesh side out
In packs of ten.
35 of them packs'd weigh 4, 5 tons,
Take six span of mules to pull.
You had a good season
You'd have maybe four loads like that.

Hadda be careful how you handled 'em though.
Don't get it right and you'd lose
3 outta 4 to bugs or rain.
Even if you was careful
You'd like to lost twenty percent.

My life was waste enough!
Once U. S. Grant had before him
On his desk
A bill for my protection.
But my lobby was not strong;
He put my safety in his pocket.

> You couldn't be too quick to claim
> A carcass. Fella on the Yellowstone
> Got killed by a dead bull.
> Had already cut out the tongue
> When the shaggy head swung round,
> A perfect arc of horn, an
> Spilled his innards in the sand.
>
> The railroads gave us plenty chance
> For sport! Train and game both
> Humping along fifteen miles a hour,
> All the sports whanging away
> Fifty guns a crack . . .
> Ten dollars would take you
> To the end of the line.

Yes! End of my line too!

> Well, they was plenty a them;
> We all thought so,
> Could watch 'em cross yer path
> And never believe
> They was an end in sight.
> When Coronado come through here
> He walked three months
> Across these prairies an wrote,
>   "I found so many cattle,"
> (He called buffs cattle),
>   "it should be impossible to estimate
>   their numbers.
>   There was not a single day
>   from my departure till return
>   when I lost sight of them."

Men fought over us—
Crazy Woman Creek,
Wagon Box, the Hayfield—
Fetterman died for us,
Adobe Walls, Crook on Rosebud,
Custer on Washita,

The Little Big Horn . . .
All in vain
The slaughter of men
Would not stop the slaughter
Of animals.
The men in blue wanted our death,
Sheridan begged for it;
Used our death to bring the tribes
Another way of dying.

1820
The real professionals take to the field
And work my northern herd.
By 1825
Over the whole prairie
North and south
My hides are tanned and stacked
Like a fever mounting.
212,000 of my hides are shipped every year
From 1835 till 1840.

> *Even Hickock tried it!*
> *Never met the man myself*
> *But Mari says he took a turn,*
> *'Bout 67, think it was.*
> *Lost his hides to Indians.*
> *Nearly lost his own skin too!*
> *Finally figured drunken cowboys*
> *Was safer'n angry Indians,*
> *So he took up other things.*
> *Bein "Wild Bill"*
> *Seemed easier I suppose.*

In '72
Ten thousand men, maybe 20
Are on the plains
Set to slaughter me.
They do it very well –
From all over the prairie
Farther than we can see from here
One million four hundred ninety one thousand
Hides are shipped, empty hides
Migrating across the plains
On the backs of trains, skinned flesh
Moving east, a great herd dead and stripped
And dried and jerked.

One million five hundred eight thousand
Shipped out in '73.

And in the north again
In '76
Eighty thousand of my kind
Shipped from Ft. Benton alone.

> *You bet they hunted*
> *For the white trade.*

I fed the tribes of this land
Thousands of years.
We had an agreement!

> *Them Blackfeet kill 15, 20 thousand*
> *Ever year for a while, all for the trade.*
> *Crows, Gros Ventres, Assiniboin*
> *All did the same.*

To make my people come
Hidatsa have a dance.
Six old men made up like bulls
Sing and dance as best they can.
Old men without any teeth
Pretending to eat my meat,
Wiping their mouths and laughing
To show how pleased they'll be
When their magic
Brings our herds again.

We know this to be true.
They tried everything against us!
Their magic!

> *Well, the Sioux, Cheyenne, 'Rapahoe, Pawnee all*
> *Bring in another 60,000 more.*
> *Indians alone took in 400,000 hides*
> *In '73. Fact, from 1850 to 1860*
> *Indians kill about three and a half*
> *Million*
> *Ever year.*

With the word between us
Broken, they turned on me
With all the determination
Of White men

Bent on commerce.
Both of us were doomed thereby.

> *Yeah, we sold it all,*
> *Fat and tongues too.*
> *They bought the fat for candles.*
> *Hadda ship the tongues in brine,*
> *An that was some mess*
> *Organizin that.*

By '72
The pickers came to take my bones.
The Santa Fe in '73 shipped
Two million seven hundred forty thousand pounds
Of bones.

> *The winter of '80-'81,*
> *That was some winter!*
> *Everbody gets good stands.*
> *Jim McNaney is just a kid nineteen*
> *But he gets 91 in one stand.*
> *A hunderd miles N.E. of Miles*
> *Vic Smith get 107*
> *In one hour!*
> *Doc Aughl kills 85*
> *An never moves from his spot.*
> *John Edwards gets 75 . . .*

> *1881*
> *There was still maybe*
> *500,000 buffalo within*
> *A hunderd and fifty miles of Miles City,*
> *Still about a million*
> *In the northern herd.*

This was the way
Of my going

> *Springtime '82*
> *Them hunters come up like buttercups*
> *On the prairies—5000 of them*
> *Just between the big bend of the Missouri*
> *An the Idaho line.*

Like an old plough
Auctioned cheap and
Going!

October through February
That same year
Just about takes 'em all.
Come late spring in '83
75,000 cross the Yellowstone;
Our boys get 'em all but about 5000
In less'n a month,

Going!

Poor George! Mari says
He sunk 8, 10 thousand dollars
In a outfit that year. Set up camp
Right there, just like the big boys done,
Same place buffalo'd blacked the prairie
Ever year anybody could remember.
He was a year too late.

Gone!

Just three seasons
We stripped that herd;
Killed one million five hunderd thousand
Buffalo.
They brought 4,500,000 dollars American
An that ain't chickenfeed.

So now I'll live
On ranches and reservations,
Be bred with cows
To meet the needs of commerce
Once again.

With a special permit
You can hunt me still;
I'll give myself to you
Hide and horns and hoofs
And all. And

One more thing
Before I go—
You called me stupid
Because I ran from fire,
Let myself be driven
Before the shouts of warriors,
Or got confused by hunters
On a stand . . .

At least I kept you
Warm and wealthy—no, not those
Who hunted me or picked my bones,
But you who banked the profits
East of St. Louis—
I made you rich,
You let me die
And called it square.
But—No hard feelings!
Come round again,
We'll talk some more . . .
When you know yourselves
As well as I know me and mine,
Let's talk again.

Perhaps we'll find
A better word
And in some future now,
If there are any of either of us,
Perhaps we'll come
To some new term
And try once more
To build a word between us
And start anew—
What's left of me,
What's left of you—

Agreed?

VIII. THE SOUND OF THE SNAPPING GUIDON

Frontier service meant abominable food and living conditions, grinding monotony punctuated at infrequent intervals by the hardest and least rewarding kind of field duty, long separation from friends and family and the comforts of civilization, and the prospect of death or disability from disease, enemy action, or a constitution broken by exposure and improper diet. It meant low pay, little chance for advancement or personal recognition, and for enlisted personnel harsh, often brutal discipline."

> Robert M. Utley
> *The Frontier Army*
> *1848-1861*

If you want a man to keep his head when the crisis comes, you must give him some training before it comes."

> Seneca
> *Letter XVIII*

War is the father of us all and our king . . .
It must be seen clearly that war is the natural state of man. . . ."

> Heraklitos
> *fragments 25, 26*

SNAPPING GUIDONS

Now
From this high place
On Rampart Range
See the Army
Moving out below us,
Forerunner and protector
Of settlers and commerce . . .

Scouts
Out ahead of everyone,
Out all night if need be,
Probing the country for sign,
Ten men on horseback moving
Just below the ridges,
Wary as magpies,
Watchful as antelope.

Then over the horizon
The pioneer detail
Comes into view;
Handful of men
Making trails for the long
Blue line to follow,
Picking the best route,
Caving in the steep
Sides of gullies;
Far ahead of the column,
Vulnerable to attack, they work
To make an easier path
For men and horses.

Next
The main line,
Guidon staffs in the stirrups,
Guidons snapping in the prairie wind
Like tendons snapping in the knees of troopers
Old and arthritic at 35
Marching in the cold and rain;
Like bones snapping under a war axe,
Guidons fluttering in the wind
That stirs the dust that clogs
The nose, and grates behind the eyes
And never seems to die here
In this land where men die

So easily no one seems to notice;
No one to know or tell the way
Of a man's going.

Columns of two or
Columns of four when the terrain permits,
Thin blue ribbon strung out
Across these high plains
        "A skeleton crawling,"
Utley calls it,
Ranks decimated by declaration of Congress,
By death and by disease,
Bones composed of
        "Bummers, loafers, and foreign paupers,"
Fleshed out with
        "Criminals, brutes, and drunkards."

Senior officers head the main column,
Cavalry next,
Infantry behind the horses
Choking on the dust,
Then wheeled vehicles —
        the artillery
        supply wagons
        light ambulance —

Flank and rear guards
Well away from the main column,
Watchful and bored,
Tired eyes squinting against the sun and dust
Or slitted against the rain,
Sticky with windblown sleet.

Look past the stars of officers,
The bars and oak leaves,
See the driven, the desperate
Enlisted, sliding down the mud walls
Of ravines, ankles twisting
Under the heavy packs, cold in winter
For lack of clothes, sweating through
The regulation wool underwear
Required to be worn the blast furnace
Days of summer; walking the miles
In split-leather shoes made in Leavenworth
Or shoddy boots that pain the feet and

"Appear to have this objection,"
The general reported,
        "The soles are fastened to the uppers
        by oval brass screws, which arrangement
        it was thought, was a great advantage,
        but it is found that the screws will
        work through the sole in long marches
        and wound the feet."

The enlisted living
On hardtack and coffee,
Beans when they're lucky,
Though
        "It is believed that a decently
        provided table, equal to that
        which most working men in the
        country have, could be supplied
        without additional cost,"
According to the general, reporting to Congress,
But such a meal was never provided
At any cost . . .
Watch this pageant
Moving below us —
The marching into this country,
The cutting of wood
For the building of posts,
The cutting of hay
For the feeding of stock,
The hauling of water,
Posting of orders
Establishing the routine . . .

The enlisted watching
Every step to obey
The endless regulations
And avoid the discipline
Of an officer's anger.
Even John Ryan, an officer
Kind as most, had a man
Hung by his wrists from a rafter
In the barn, twisting all night
For cutting a halter.
The reprimand meant a day
In the guardhouse and others
On sick list. He was lucky.

Might have been staked
Out in the sun and flies,
        "Spread eagle,"
As Rickey describes it,
Or doubled up,
        "Bucked and gagged,"
        (wrists bound to ankles,
        unable to move),
Then left in the snow or sun
So long one soldier
Found his comrade
        "Unconscious, eyes wide open
        and staring. . . ."

        "Do you recollect,"
Ryan wrote in 1908,
        "the large hole General Custer
        had dug in the ground at Camp Sturgis,
        on the side of the hill where the guardhouse was
        where we used to put prisoners at night?
        I was Sergeant of the Guard there
        the day that there came very near being a riot. . . ."

There was death for desertion
        (But flogging more often)
Or a shaved head
And a big "D"
Branded on the butt, to go
With a drumming from the post.

See these sad enlisted
Suffering the deadly post
Routine, the off-post details
That light a candle of fear
In the gut, a flickering that never goes
Out, even years later, retired and back east,
Fear that makes a man twitch and roll
Suddenly in his sleep, remembering
The forced marches with too little
Food, too little equipment,
Too little ammunition;
Too much bad weather,
Too heavy packs,
Too many Indians . . .

Enduring the intricate Sunday ritual
Of Full Dress Inspection,
White gloves on the guns, the brass;
The Sunday ceremony to sanctify
The security of the post,
The obedience of men,
The Sabbath, and the routine
The routine, the routine, the routine . . .
See too
How they go to war
With the people who inhabit this land;
How quickly the blood of these men
Soaks into my prairie soil,
Runs in the creeks and rivers
Of this country;
How the bodies bloat, turn black,
Surrender to beasts and rain, the white
Bones scattering across the plains
From the mouths of rodents and carnivores;
How blood stains the past, the present,
Taints this future we face now.

Watch this Army
Moving on this land.
These men, too, have come from me
And will return to me.
I am Earth, and I am
Open to my sons
Of every kind.

ON THE TRAIL

My dear Nordene,

Have just returned to the post
from our most recent, and pointless,
pursuit of hostiles, to find your letter
waiting. I was glad to hear about the boys,
& to know you & the farm are fine.

You asked again how it is out here.
Life on the trail is far from simple,
& probably not the way most folks think.
We are up before 5:00 & our days
ricochet from bugler to shouted commands

to shuffling dust or slippery mud
& back again. The schedule is nearly
firm as it would be back at the post.

First Call
Comes at
4:45

At
4:55 comes
Reveille & Stable Call.
How the commands echo
in the thin summer dawning.
Come to Order!
     Saddle up!
Harness mules!
Stock inspection! the Sergeants bawl.
We must complete our chores
before the breakfast mess.

5:00
Mess Call!
We prepare our own
& breakfast rarely varies.
We have beef hash, dry sliced bread
without butter, coffee without milk.
The coffee they give us is beans
which I wrap in a rag and grind
with the butt of my rifle.

5:30
General Quarters!
We strike our tents & store
our gear for travel.

5:45
Boots and Saddles!
Cavalry mount your horses!

5:55
Fall in!
We form a line of march,
still hooking things on our belts
and organizing our gear.

6:00
The commander calls

"Forward March!"
And we begin to move.
The custom may change
with a change in commanders.
Crook and Custer are deadly
on the trail. With them the men
hit the prairie all strung out
at 3:00 A.M.

This time we march
till 11 in the morning
then break to rest our livestock.
We are forbidden fires
for the noon meal,
so we jaw mightily against
sliced beef & dry bread
or hardtack & salt pork,
and wash it down with cold coffee
left over from breakfast.

At 1:00 P.M.
we resume march,
the only sounds the sounds of our feet,
rustle of clothes or leather,
jangle of tin cups dangling from haversacks or belts.
Each man works on his walking.
Some adopt a trance-like demeanor,
eyes fixed on the trail, counting steps in time
to keep the legs moving. The trick is to empty
the mind, forget the working body,
and narrow the vision to the moving feet.
At times we become almost disembodied, not feeling
the feet hit the ground, so preoccupied we float.
Each man wrapped thus in his own counsel,
nobody talks.

There's nothing to talk about anyway,
marching,
        "Even if there was,"
says Bourke (you remember Bourke)
            "conversation would have flagged.
            Your old soldier is a taciturn, grumpy
·   animal on the march,
                not much given to an expression
                of opinion on any topic."

The trail is a duty
hard on horses as it is on us.
  "After the fourth day's march
  of a mixed command
  the horse does not march
  faster than the foot soldier,"
Colonel Hazen claims, and
  "after the seventh day
  the foot soldier begins
  to outmarch the horse."
From then on we have to end our march
earlier and earlier each day
just to let the cavalry get to camp
the same day we do.

& Finerty once wrote to his paper,
  "We used to joke
  about the infantry,"
but he acknowledges that finally,
  "we recognized that man is
  a hardier animal than the horse
  and that shank's mare is the very
  best kind of charger."
We surely enjoyed reading that.
Finerty is better than most, & it is
always nice to see a correspondent
pay some attention to the foot soldier.

At 4:00 P.M.
we break march & tackle our chores:
  set up picket line for horses & mules
  feed and water stock
  post guards
  send out fuel and water details
  raise tents
and then have our evening meal:
  hardtack and coffee.
After that we have time
for cards, conversation, letters home,
clowning & music. We know
tomorrow's the same
unless it rains, hails,
sleets or snows, and we get soaked
or frozen.

Often
when the patrol is more
than routine
we'll march till midnight
in pursuit of hostiles,
move out again at 3:00 A.M.
stumbling in darkness and fatigue.
Fear takes our feet
out from under us
on the edge of the wash,
and the men curse the cold,
the dark, the trail, the army
& some curse the life
that got them into this —
the woman back home they'd go
through this to get away from,
the gambling debt or dead man
that forced their flight
into another name, another place.

But you know
I am here, not for any such
reasons as those
but duty . . .

Tell Arnold, Jr., to be sure
he takes care of chores
and make little Edward
a man for me,

Yr. faithful husband,

    Arnold

P.S. I am enclosing a clipping,
nearly a year late in reaching us &
badly handled, but it tells pretty
much what a skirmish is like out here.

    A.

FINERTY AND KING
REPORT THE ATTACK

At eight P.M.
we glide in among the timbers;
at nine we are bivouacked,
horses and men
in a great circle under the bluffs.
We have marched eighty-five miles
in thirty-one hours,
but no fires are lighted
as we wait in the dark.

"And now
my Indian friends
riding out of the silence
what of you?

"Savage warfare was never
more beautiful than in you,
your swift ponies springing
down the winding ravine,
the rising sun gleaming
on your trailing bonnets,
on silver armlets,
on necklace or gorget,
on painted shield and beaded legging,
on naked body and beardless face.

"Swaying in all the wild grace
of your horsemanship,
twenty seconds and you will appear
around that point!
Two hundred yards now,
I can hear the panting
of your wiry horses!

"I hold vengeance in my hand
but not yet to let it go!"

Ten seconds more!
A hundred yards—ninety!
        "Now, lads, in with you!"
Crash of hoofs!
Rush of dust and noise.
        "Drive in, Mason!"

Wheeling, backing, firing!
        "Look out for the main ridge!"
Advancing, falling!
          "Murphy!"

In a bright tumult of sound and light
we are pitched
headlong into perfect vision,
indelible cameos of clarity and violence,
bunching muscles, an open mouth
focused in a roaring periphery
of dust and confusion . . .

Then the deadly racket becoming
sporadic,
fading at the retreat of color and muscle
and we can really see again.

It is late afternoon.
The hospital is established
in the trees
down by the sluggish creek,
the surgeons' matchless steel
nerves flaring
in the slant of light.

We sit where we are in the open,
exhausted, slumped in the sudden silence
and the sun,
our minds an emptying riot
unable to grasp.

      "We have used up our rations
      and 25,000 rounds."

The bodies are brought in
nearly all black from the heat.
A grave is dug for the dead
in the bed of the dry stream.

After the bodies are covered
we ride
back and forth over them;
we lift up our eyes
unto the hills
and see the rest of the troops

straggling out over the rim
of the valley
headed for the post.

PARADE REST

Dear Nordene,
Glad for yrs of the 10th.
& to know the children are well,
& you. Are the beans now in?
& the squash?

In reply to yr questions about Army
life, this is the way it is with us
in the Department of the Missouri:

Sometimes I swear
the post routine is
even more deadly than being on the trail.
Although we wake a little later, the schedule
is less flexible, the routine less bearable.

At 5:30 A.M.
Reveille!
The morning gun sounds
& we stumble out in the dark and cold
of winter, feet stamping, hands swatting
biceps. Our white breath hisses through
clenched teeth as we answer roll call.

6:15
First Drill!

7:00
Mess Call!

7:30
Fatigue Duty!
      The off-post details for
road building, bridge repair, wood cutting,
telegraph maintainence, escort for recruits
or paymasters, mail carriers or emigrant trains.
In summer we go for water, in winter saw ice.
These are hard labor details, & dangerous. Our
groups are always small, occupied, easy to
surprise and cut off from the post. I admit to
some fear each time we go.

The on-post details are unsavory &
onerous, but easier. Garbage and gardens,
stable clean up, parade ground police &
kitchen police.

8:30
Guard Mount!
Our most elaborate moment of the day,
music and marching, the ritual courtesy
as we transfer command.

At 12:00
Noon break!

1:00
Afternoon Fatigue!

4:30
Drill!
But this is a curious kind of drill.
Often enough it runs like this:
        "Skip the drill!"
(There's never enough men to get the rest
of the work done),
        "Better let 'em work!"

So we skip horsemanship,
skip target practice
(ammunition's too expensive).
        "Sure, you can shoot, Lieutenant,
        if you insist,"
they told one officer,
        "but the cost of every cartridge
        comes out of your paycheck!"

I remember in '66,
surrounded by Sioux and Cheyenne,
18th Infantry
held no target practice all year.
        "No wonder,"
Utley says,
        "they were poor marksmen,
        and in horsemanship
        but clumsy children
        compared with Indians."

Even now when target practice is required,
we are still limited. They issue our sergeant
twenty rounds per man per month. Supply said,
    "That's it . . . Shoot 'em any time you want—
    one a day a five day week
    or five an hour four times a month.
    Don't care how you do it, just make 'em
    marksmen!"

By 8:15 it's Taps.
In our rooms we sleep two
in a bed. My bunky and I
listen to the rats
in the walls, crossing the floor
& I think about spiders, vermin
crawling in the dark.
In the summer
we drag our blankets outside
on a clear night.

Even the officers
fight the housing,
making the most of makeshift.
Last winter
Lieutenant Grummond and his bride
at Fort Phil Kearney
tacked blankets around the bed
hoping cloth walls would help
hold the heat, & covered the kitchen
windows with old newspapers.
Ollie Knight used to visit over there
& he says they covered the spuds
with a buffalo robe and put them
in the living room near the stove
each night before they went to bed.
Of course the milk froze, but that winter
would freeze milk still in the udder.

& I guess the nights got even colder
for Mrs. Grummond. Her husband
was with Fetterman, you know.
They found him in the rocks
up on Lodge Trail Ridge.

But rank, as always, has its privileges.
Knight says a senior officer can always turn

a junior out of his house on the basis of rank.
But he can only do that once, when he first
moves in, unless someone of higher rank
comes along and wants his place, then everyone
below has to move again. We call it
"Tumbling bricks."

About the only relief
for boredom is the chance
to go into the field.
But you know of life on the trail.
How strange! We are almost willing to trade
a threat to life for a change in routine . . .

Once the monotony of our military
meals was relieved by a feast on Christmas.
At Fort Smith we had a real feed,
honest to God fowl. The officers
even had pâté. The cook pretended to be
a "French chef," & things got pretty
fancy for a time!
Of course the fowl was sage hen we hunted
ourselves, & the pâté was venison,
& the chef was just a striker
with a mysterious past.

My friend, "Frontier," is really sour.
He writes letters to his hometown newspaper
& in July he wrote,
           "Of all the dull and unendurable lives
           the one of the soldier on the plains
           is the worst. It is just dragging out
           a miserable existence."

While I do not mind it
as much as he, it is tough, dull duty
right enough. But, as old Jim used to say,
           "Even a blind sow will find a few
           acorns in the wintertime."

And now I must close.
Hold my young ones close
for me, & yourself.

        Yrs.

        Arnold.

HORSES AND MULES

My Dear Wife,

This country & this life are just a shade
our side of intolerable, or would be
if there were any shade & combat holds a
special misery for horses as for men.
Wounded animals are human in their suffering
& in the attachments we form for them. Ran
into Nevin last month and he told me of a
friend of his whose horse was shot. He wrote
Davey,

> "I found that Sam was shot through
> the bowels. I unsaddled him and turned
> him loose to die, but he followed me
> like a dog and would put his head against
> me and push, groaning like a person. I
> was forced to shoot him to end his misery.
> I had to try two or three times before I
> could do it. He kept looking at me with
> his great brown eyes. When I did fire
> he never knew what hurt him. He was a
> splendid horse, and could do his mile
> in 1.57."

Out here a good horse is worth your life,
a bad one can kill you sure as Indians.

Caspar Collins had a horse we all knew to be
hard headed, with a habit of running away.
Spring told us Caspar was shot in the hip
as he rode down a hill, but even the soldier
riding next to him could not tell if it was
serious, for the Lieutenant said nothing of it.

When they reached the bottom Caspar turned
back for a wounded man who was on foot. He
managed to raise the man, partially, but his
horse became unmanageable and whirled,
dancing away, breaking into a run that carried
Caspar to the center of a crowd of Indians
where he was overwhelmed and lost to view, his
life made forfeit to a headstrong horse. He
was a good officer and seemed a fine man.
Getting his name left on a prairie town
seems a small memorial.

Mules are as important as horses. Though
cantankerous and noisy, they are strong
packers and reliable transport. Many scouts
and civilian frontiersmen prefer them for
strength and bottom and use them for their
regular mounts. & the "prairie canary,"
as the men call them, has a special music,
which Bourke says may be

> "Just a particle monotonous
> and the nasal pitch he commonly employs
> somewhat harsh for cultivated ears,
> but the question of pitch
> is a question of taste
> and the mule's taste may be better
> than our own—or, if worse,
> this is the land of liberty
> and the mule is free to enjoy himself
> as he pleases . . .

> "The charge of monotony is true,
> but it applies with equal force
> to the song of the lark, which
> we all pretend to admire."

Enough for now. My love to the boys,
& to you.

> Arnold

HARDTACK AND HEALTH

Dear Nordene,

Just a little more about life out here.
If we are lucky, it will soon be possible
for me to come back home.

Meanwhile you are not to worry. I complain,
but so do we all. We eat dull food, but
plenty. And some of it, like hardtack,
which is the butt of many gripes, has also
become something of a joke.

You'd think we could eat it, it is so perfectly
made—each little rectangle always 3 & 1/8

inches by 2 & 7/8th inches by 1/2 inch thick.
Like our schedule, it is militarily precise
and perfectly unpalatable, light brown
& baked so brittle the crumbs turn to dust
fine ground. The men call them "flour tiles,"
for they are almost impossible to swallow.
We think they can turn a bullet, almost!
And a stomach surely.
There was a trooper Nevin knew
who got a tile so dark & stale,
so hard, that when he bit it
his teeth could not even make an
impression. So, he says,

> "Holding it in the palm
> of my left hand,
> I struck it with my right fist,
> but only succeeded
> in skinning my knuckles.
>
> "Tried to break it
> by holding it with both hands
> twisting as I used to do
> to break apples. It resisted.
>
> "Then I brought it down
> several times, hard,
> on my knee—
> but only bruised my knee!"

On the bluffs with Reno
we used it for breastworks.

> "Stack her up, boys,"

the sergeant yelled,

> "If that won't turn a bullet
> nothing will . . .
> If we're held here too long
> before Terry comes,
> we can eat the breastworks, boys!"

One of the men yelled back,

> "Hey, Sarge,
> let's feed it to the Indians instead!
> You want to subdue the wild Indian,
> feed 'em our hardtack!"

We have no fruit, no vegetables, but plenty
of hardtack and scurvy,
cholera, flue, diptheria, yellow fever,
smallpox and typhoid. All our posts
lose more men to sickness
than to Indians. Once 700 men got
cholera & half of them died, and once
7000 got dysentery, though only 151 died.

The commander at Ft. Stevenson
over in Dakota Territory reports
that of the 200 men in his post
51 are down with scurvy
and one has died.
Doc says one man in 33 dies each year
either from disease or the curing of it.

The Sergeant loves to torment us:

> "Whiskey and quinine
> is the cure, boys!
> Some here for every ailment.
> More powerful the purgative
> the better!"

No mail today, nor for five weeks now
& I do not know when this will go.
Kiss the boys for me. I hope you are able to
stay well and happy.

Yr. loving husband,

Arnold

COLD

Dear Wife,

This winter seems especially hard
and cold. Nevin was laughing this
morning because his bunky was wearing

> "Two flannels and buckskin shirt;
> one pair of drawers,
> buckskin trousers, Army trousers,
> two pair woolen socks; big boots,
> buffalo overshoes, a heavy pair

of blanket leggings;
thick blouse, heavy overcoat;
a woolen cap . . ."

which covered his head, face & neck,
except for the nose and eyes. He could
hardly move for the clothes, & it would
seem he should have been warm, but
Nevin says he reported,

"Still I am not happy."

Often our weather has been more serious.
Two of our men went hunting last week.
One froze so bad he fell off his horse
and died during the night. His partner
stayed with him till morning, then tried
to get back to the post. We found him a
few miles out, snow blind and froze in
all the extreme parts. His partner we
found curled like a ball against the
belly of his horse, and had to throw him
in the wagon still circled up like that.
When we got back with him we discovered
that his partner had died too. We buried
them both this afternoon.

Bourke says one of the most disagreeable
days he ever put in was Christmas in '76,
trying to get into bivouac in the Pumpkin
Buttes:

"Beards, moustaches, eyelashes and
eyebrows were frozen masses of ice.
The keen air was filled with minute
crystals, each cutting the tender skin
like a razor, while feet and hands ached
as if beaten with clubs. Horses and
mules shivered while they stood in
column, their flanks white with crystals
of perspiration congealed on their bodies,
and their nostrils bristling with icicles.

"Two of our thermometers indicated 26
degrees below zero, Fahrenheit . . .
Spirit glasses in Deadwood registered
that day 40 degrees below, and in Fort

Sanders, Wyoming, 58 degrees below zero,
Fahrenheit, and we were in direct line
of the blast howling between those two
points."

But I do not mean to tell too much
& you must not fear for me.
I write these things
only to remember.
I escape most difficulties
& can still send you this
from your loving husband.

   Yrs. Faithfully,

   Arnold

PAYDAY

My Dearest Nordene,

Payday is here again. You might
think it is a regular thing, but out
here deliveries of all kinds are
irregular & sometimes we go two, or
even six or eight months without a
payday.

Old timers remember that before '54
infantry and artillery were paid $7.00
per month, Cavalry $8.00 & the
Sergeants got $13.00.

However small the amount, there is generally
enough for a drink & a fight, though sometimes
you owe a whole payday to the sutler's before
payday ever comes. Then it is merely depressing.

My friend, "Frontier," wrote in
his newspaper,

"The paymaster (Major Burbank) made his
appearance on his bi-monthly visit to the
garrison on the 27th ultimo. The most of the
money went to the sutler's for 'red-eye,' and
consequences are a number of cases in the
hospital, broken heads, black eyes, and twelve
cases for court-martial."

It's common to punish such offenses by
making the men carry logs weighing twenty
or thirty pounds, round and round the stockade
for fifteen to thirty days, depending on
the nature of the offense.

Congress raised the pay to $16.00 a month
for a while, but reduced it again in '71.
They pay us $13. now, in paper. But the
paper is scrip, and we have to convert it
to gold or silver, a task the post sutler
is happy to handle—for a slight fee
ranging from 15 to 40 percent.

The men grumble,

> "A dollar a day
> Is damn poor pay
> But 13 a month is less!"

So far I have not been able to save much
but I have managed to stay out of trouble
and away from the cards. You know I don't
drink enough to fight.

Yr. Loyal Husband,

Arnold

SOLDIERS AND SCOUTS

My Loving Wife,

Wonderful news! After one more expedition I
am to be released from this duty I had begun
to think endless. I should be home in time
for fall chores and can help with the harvest!
The boys will be so big I doubt I'll
recognize them. Though life out here
is mostly terribly dull, I will have some
stories to tell!

I have written before about Custer.
I no longer believe he is a hater.
He does his job, and perhaps ruthlessly.
But Indians like to have him
present when it is time to negotiate.

His signing is superb, so he is
useful to them. If he were not worthy
of trust, I feel sure they would know
& would shun him. They trust him
to be ruthless in pursuit &
merciless in the attack, but
decent in their captivity.

I am ashamed to admit it,
but he writes to his wife even more
often than I write to you.
Hardly a day the dispatches go
without a letter to his Libby.

So I am glad to be with him again,
for even though he is tough on men
and horses, he does see that we work
to stay in shape and trains us hard
so that we may be sure of ourselves
in the field. Other officers are too
lazy or too drunk to make us work.
Custer has his critics, & probably
deserves them, but others are just
as demanding or petty, & for less
purpose and smaller reward.

Sheridan, for example.
When we are headquartered Sheridan is a
typical officer:
            lively dinner partner
            good dancer & loves theatre
            gallant companion
            & loves pretty women.
But in the field he is an unforgiving demon,
restless, irritable, relentless in pursuit
and unforgiving of his enemies. At least
he endures what we endure, & forsakes many
comforts that lesser officers demand.

            "Marching at our head in snow and rain,
            enduring all the hardships of wind and
            weather,"

is the way Bourke tells it & while that isn't
the whole story by a long shot, that part of
it is true. When the tents blew down in '68,
the general just crawled under a wagon
with the rest of us.

His orders are as hard as this hardscrabble
country, hard as anthracite under the limestone
back home. To Custer on the Washita:

"Kill or hang all warriors."

Sherman is just the same. That's what he
said too; the telegraph fairly hums with
hostility when he is on the wire:

"Kill as many as you can . . ."

he told Custer.

After the Fetterman fiasco
Sherman's pique was near hysteric.
He wired Sheridan,

"We must act with vindictive earnestness
against the Sioux, even to their extermination,
men, women, and children. Nothing less will
reach the root of this case."

The word to Custer is always the same,
perhaps because he is the only one likely
to fulfill it, the one objective clear
in every mind. The word becomes "kill,"
and lives among us along every little stream
on the front slope & will live long beyond
our day, smoldering unseen like the sparks
from a prairie fire.

Sheridan sure likes Bill Cody,
and no wonder. Cody rode for him the winter
of '68:

65 miles from Ft. Larned to Ft. Hays,
the route, "infested with Indians."
From Hays, Cody rode 95 miles to Ft. Dodge.
"Several couriers had been killed along
that stretch," the dispatches said.
From Ft. Dodge back to Ft. Larned &
from Larned back to Hays—he rode 350
miles in 60 hours carrying messages.

That's something to remember
when others call him fraud & showman only.
He's stylish all right, but on this frontier
there are so many frauds you have to be good

even to be a fraud of note. Captain King
says of all the scouts he ever knew,

> "Cody was the paragon . . . beautiful
> horseman, unrivalled shot, unequaled
> scout,"

& as he says,

> "We have tried them all!"

One time when Cody wasn't around
Charley White announced himself to Sheridan
saying,

> "I'm Buffalo Bill
> when Bill's away!"

Sheridan replied,

> "The hell you are;
> you're buffalo s_____!"

But most of us liked Charley & called him
"Buffalo Chips." We liked him even though
he was a bit of a clown, & we were sad when
he was killed. Finerty was there when he
got shot. He told us Charley took a bullet
right in the chest, and he said,

> "My God, my God, boys,
> I'm done for this time!"

then convulsed, stiffened, and rolled
like a log down the slope, wind blowing his
long fair hair over the cold face, eyes dead,
but not quite closed.

Sheridan thinks George Crook is decent
and humane, but I am not sure he admires
those qualities in a General. Bourke is
a great admirer of Crook, too much so for
my taste, & once he called Crook

> "A beacon of hope to the settler,
> a terror to the tribes in hostility."

Sheridan hates the ostrich-feather hat
Crook wears for the photos, and likes even
less the pith helmet & white stable-detail
coveralls Crook wears to war. Makes him

look too much like a "government ghost,"
& as if he cares more for his men than
Sheridan does.

But that Crook! He does not smoke or drink,
even coffee! And I've never heard him swear.
In fact in the field he's hardly every heard
at all! Most closed mouthed man I ever saw,
but Finerty says,

> "His eyes could swear a gallon."

He seems to be thoughtful and imaginative
and believes our enemies to be human. He
deals honorable with his foes, or tries to,
& I like that. But in reports he can twist
the truth with the best of defenders
of sorry careers—the Reno's or Benteens . . .

Sheridan said he's soft on Indians,
then called him north to serve against
the Sioux.

Crook despises Sheridan's cruelty,
once called him,

> "That bloated little carcass,"

then went north to kill Indians.

And now I am going too. When we are through
I'll be happy to return to you and our boys.

> Yrs. Faithfully,

> Arnold

P.S. Be sure the boys do not lollygag, but
learn to like to work.

> A.

IX. REPORT OF THE COMMISSION: WE HAVE AN AGREEMENT

N°, Cap, it's not the right way to give um presents to buy peace; but if I was governor of these yeer United States, I'll tell you what I'd do. I'd invite um all to a big feast, and make believe I wanted to have a big talk; and as soon as I got um altogether I'd pitch in and sculp about half of um, and then t'other half would be mighty glad to make a peace that would stick. That's the way I'd make a treaty with the dog'ond, red-bellied varmints; and as sure as you're born, Cap, that's the only way."
    Jim Baker Randolph B. Marcy's
    The Prairie Traveler

What Nature forbids is that we should increase our own means, property and resources by plundering others. . . ."
    Cicero
    On Duties

The contest that should be for truth and virtue is for sway and belongings instead."
    Diogenes
    fragment 51

AMERICA THE AMBIVALENT

"But Pompey bids Right a long farewell,
and is off to Brundisium."
> Cicero
> *Letter to Atticus*
> 24 February, 49 B.C.

Now from this high place
See below us
Plains and rivers, the dry grass,
People indigenous
And people new to this country
Come together in a United State;
That state growing and moving,
A trickle becoming a torrent:
> America the Ambivalent,
> First Nation of Democracy,
Moving west; nation of faces,
Of masks . . .

> Half-man mask;
> One half human,
> The other half—
> Human too!
> One half dark,
> One half light,
> But one mask!

Behind it
> One face
> One body
> One people
Hunter and farmer one,
Gatherer and grocer one,
Crazy Horse and Custer one
The People divided
> The People indivisible
The People all related
> The People all one!

See them
Strike agreements with one another,
Establish a word, not always
    understood,

Nevertheless a word between them
Agreed to long as the grass shall grow
Long as the rivers flow.

And hear this nation say,

> "Of course agreements
> are subject to change,
> not expected to hold.
> Exigencies will arise . . ."

We will discover gold,
A railroad is required;
The land we took
And then gave back reduced
We need again

> "In the national interest . . ."

The national interest the same
                as Northern Pacific's interest
                Anaconda's interest

> "Indeed we have our national honor!
>   (Our national interest more)
> "We seek a boon for all concerned,
> and ask your land again, once more.
> Your own best interest will be served
>   (and ours as well).
> Provide us with your land
> and we'll provide for you . . .

Strip your life of meaning
And call you shiftless too,

> "You surely do agree. . . ."

See these agreements,
The words between us
Made and broken,
And remember:
I am Earth
But I can be broken too.
Break the word
And you break me.

Enough.

WE HAD AN AGREEMENT
ABOUT LAND

The Fourth Annual Report
Of the Indian Commission
To the President of the United States
1872

Mr. President,

". . . Their lands were not
conveyed to them
as an act of grace,
but for considerations
deemed of ample value
by the Government;

nor can their rights
be properly affected
by the question whether
they are White, or Red.

The greed for gold and land
causes its rapacious subjects
to overrun the reservations
of the Cheyennes and Arapahoes
when the ink of the treaty
which guaranteed possession
is hardly yet dried on the paper.

And with no provocation proved,
a regiment of volunteers
perpetrate the infamous
Sand Creek Massacre.

The consequent war costs
hundred of lives,
the depopulation of the border,
and thirty million dollars. . . ."

THE GOVERNMENT SEEKS
AN AGREEMENT WITH THE SIOUX
ON BEHALF OF AMERICAN INDUSTRY
AND IN THE NATIONAL INTEREST

". . . It was greatly the desire of the Board
that an amicable agreement should be had
with the Sioux and other Indians
before the commencement of surveys
through their hunting grounds.
Without such agreement, it was to be expected
that some of these warlike bands, jealous
of encroachment of the whites upon
the territories they claim, and opposed
to the construction of the railroad,
which will banish or destroy the game
from which they derive their food, clothing
and shelter, would attempt forcible resistance.

"The surveys were commenced,
owing to the exigencies of the case, as we suppose,
previous to the negotiation with the Indians,
and the surveying parties
met with some opposition . . .

"The visit of Hon. B. R. Cowen,
has resulted in inducing a number of chiefs
to visit Washington.
It is hoped their observations,
added to such judicious measures
as may be adopted during the winter and spring,
will convince them they will be dealt with
justly and humanely by the Government,
as well as of the futility of war,
and prevent any serious resistance
to the construction of the road."

WE ARE AGREED:
THERE WILL BE OUTRAGES

"That outrages by individual Indians
or small bands
will occur, is likely.
That outrages upon the Indians
will be committed by desperadoes

among the whites
is to be expected,
and that such cases, should they occur,
will be made use of by interested parties
and others opposed to the peace policy
to provoke war
is also certain."

THE GOVERNMENT SEEKS
TO ALTER AN AGREEMENT
WITH THE CROWS

". . . The Crow reservation is large,
and the western boundary follows
the east bank of the Yellowstone
from the mouth of the first canyon
to the edge of the National Park,
about sixty miles.

"Should the Northern Pacific Railroad
adopt the Yellowstone route,
travel to the White Mountain Hot Springs,
soon destined to recognition
as one of the wonders of the world,
and the National Park, will diverge
near the mouth of the canyon,
and follow the western bank of the river,
and the beautiful and fertile valleys
between the canyons will be quickly populated.

"This fact, soon to be realized,
and that of the mining
on the western end of the reservation,
suggest the expediency of negotiation
with the Crows for the relinquishment
of part of their land.

"Should Congress not deem the negotiation
expedient, or should it fail,
there is no other just course to pursue
than to banish the miners
from the reservation
in accordance with the treaty."

AN AGREEMENT WITH THE INDIANS
AT FORT BERTHOLD AGENCY

General Sully reports:

". . . They have a treaty with the Government
by which they, along with other nations,
get a part of $50,000 every year,
but they have no idea
what that portion is,
and the treaty does not so state.
All they know is, that seven years ago
they got a very handsome present
from the Government every year,
and since that it has been growing less and less,
till this year, when their agent, M. Wilkinson,
told them they were to receive nothing.

"That commanding officer, however,
tells me that after the agent left
(for the agents for those Indians
don't live in the country, they only
visit them once a year),
twenty-four sacks of flour,
and twenty-four boxes of hard bread
reached here, directed to the agent. . . ."

MR. BRUNOT AND COLONEL VIALL
TALK TO THE BLACKFEET ABOUT HOUSES

<u>Mr. Brunot:</u>

I want to ask Little Wolf
some questions.
Have you a house now?

    <u>Little Wolf:</u>

    Yes.

Are you going to live in it
all the time?

    I cannot see where else I can go.
    I want to live in the house all the time.

Did you ever live
in a house before?

No. This is my first house.

Are you going to sow grain
and have a farm?

I am going to put seed in and farm.

Do you think these men want
houses if they can get them?

There are many who would like to have
houses. All these people do not go far
away; they would like to have houses
and work. They like these rivers and
the country and want to stay here.

Colonel Viall:

When you have your houses built, if you fear other Indians
stealing your horses,
you can build a stockade
and keep your horses in it.

It is all good.

Brunot:

A man may hear good, and say it is
good, yet he may go out of the house
and that is the end of it. I do not
want you to do this way . . .

Viall:

Last fall we talked about building your houses.
You made the same promise about living in them,
and having farms. I am glad Little Wolf and
others have houses and are living in them. I
will show you how to build houses before the winter
comes. If you help one another, soon all
can have houses and they will be more comfortable
than your teepees . . . Will you all help each other
build houses when the agent shows you how?

We are all glad to help.

My heart is glad to hear these words.
In about four moons it will be cold.
If you have houses to live in, all will
be comfortable. I will come again in

two moons, and be glad to find that all
are building houses.

> I want a floor in my house . . .

WE HAVE AN AGREEMENT:
A TREATY WITH THE CROWS

Mr. President:

The treaty with the Crow Indians
negotiated by the Peace Commission,
afterward ratified by Congress,
is exceedingly liberal in every provision,
but in hardly any of its provisions
has it ever been carried out.

> "EXAMPLE:
> Article Two. The Government of the United States shall
> keep out of the reservation all white men, and shall
> prevent any and all white men (except such as it shall
> send) from passing over it."

We have found:
A hundred white men mining
on the reservation
when the treaty was made . . .

Many more have come in since
and are living on it . . .

Prospectors and miners are coming
and going on almost all parts
of this reservation
at all times . . .
Many have brought herds of horses
and cattle on it . . .

Although the Indians have made grievous complaint
the Government has never made any effort
to carry this article into effect.

> "EXAMPLE:
> Article Three: The Government agrees to locate an agency
> and erect suitable buildings at Otter Creek. A grist-mill
> and shingle mill will be provided."

We have found:
The Otter Creek location is a good one
selected by the Indians,
named in the treaty,
with an abundance of wood and water
and surrounded by country
suitable for farming.

But for reason not known,
without the consent of the Indians
the agency was located some
forty miles away from Otter Creek
and that much nearer the white
settlements of the Gallatin Valley.

It is a point in no way suited
for the purpose—
fifteen miles from any wood,
there is no water available for irrigation,
no land available for farming.

The buildings erected
at $3000 each
are very poor and unsuited for the purpose
of any agency. They are one story,
built in the shape of a fort,
shutting out all communication
between the employees
and the village around them;
none were ceilinged, plastered,
or weather-boarded;
the carpenter-shop and blacksmith-shop
are built from funds intended
for Indian homes.

> "EXAMPLE:
> Article Five. The Government of the United States shall
> protect the Crow Nation from invasion and depredations
> by their traditional enemies, such as the Sioux."

We have found:
No effort has been made by the Government
to carry out this provision.
Every year the tribes meet
and many more of the Crows are killed.
In one affray two years ago, the Crows lost

twenty-nine braves, and last year sixteen.
In both affrays a large number of horses
were captured by the Sioux.

IN ADDITION, MR. PRESIDENT,

We have found:
The farm (100 acres) last year yielded
     1000 bushels of potatoes
     3000 bushels of turnips
     1000 bushels of wheat
     A large quantity of other vegetables.

However, there being no means
for threshing, cleaning or grinding the wheat,
it was fed with the straw to the horses and cattle.
This was a hard winter and wheat
was costing $11.00 per sack.
The year's supply of seed arrived
too late. A very small crop
is anticipated.

The day school is, comparatively,
a failure . . . No religious service
has ever been held.

The supplies delivered at the agency
seem to have been left entirely
to the good faith of the contractor,
as there is no inspection other than
that of the agent, and he was not furnished
any sample of the quality contracted for,
and has no means of knowing
whether goods delivered are below
or above the proper standard.

The annuity goods bought for 1871
did not reach there till the spring
of 1872, some did not arrive till
late as June, and some did not arrive.

There is now a large sum of money
due the Crows on account of annuities unused
during the last four years, but
it seems useless to expend funds
upon so unsuitable a place.

Bad as it is, however,
it will be rendered more so
by its proximity to the Northern Pacific
when it is built.

FURTHER,
MR. PRESIDENT,

The records show
under their present treatment
the Indians commit a smaller number
of serious crimes against the whites
than an equal number of white men
in the West
commit against each other.
These facts
seem to be but little known,
and when the telegraph announces
a white man has been killed by Indians
most persons attach guilt
to the whole race . . .

As well might they hold
the clergy and merchants of New York
personally guilty of the daily murders
committed there, and express a desire
for the extermination of such merchants
and clergy.
Therefore,

SIR,
We respectfully submit
that if the national honor requires
observance of national obligations
entered into with the strong,
how much more
with the weak.

To repudiate
either directly or by any indirection
our solemn treaty obligations
with this feeble people
would be dishonor
meriting the scorn of the civilized world.

Respectfully submitted,

The Commission

X. PRAIRIE FIRE

*H*e took the scalp of the fallen brave in a
manner that displayed perfect
workmanship. Scalping is an artistic process,
and, when neatly done, may be termed a
satanic accomplishment."
　　　John F. Finerty
　　　War-Path and Bivouac

*T*he way I looks at it they hev jist this
preference: them as don't like bein'
shot to death kin take their chances at freezin'."
　　　California Joe, scout,
　　　in George A. Custer
　　　My Life on the Plains

*I*t is through earth we perceive earth, water
through water, aether through bright
aether, consuming fire through fire, love through
love, and hate through grim hate."
　　　Empedocles
　　　fragment 109

*Y*ou will sooner find a fragment of earth
unrelated to the rest of earth, than a
man without some link with his fellows."
　　　Marcus Aurelius
　　　Meditations
　　　Book Nine, 9

LAMENT

Now
Below us in the distance
The great streams
Become men, long lines
Of canvas and freight,
Of military, blue
And dusty on horseback
Or walking through the short grass,
The mountain men and war chiefs,
Men from Sandia and Eden Valley
Come together with the men
From Troy and Rome;
Brothers before history,
Now unknown to one another
As Oedipus was
Unknown to his father
At the fork in the road,
They gather in this sacred place
Where the agreements cannot hold,
Will not hold,
And stubborn men will spill
The blood of brothers
And sacrifice their own
To see who shall have me.

North
Under the lush green hills
That rise to the Big Horns,
See the leaves turn
Aspen yellow in the fall,
A quick wind taking them down;
The late rains turning to snow,
December surrounds Fort Phil Kearny
As darkness settles around a fire
In the midst of winter.

There below us
In the fort
Is Captain Fetterman
His mind cold enough
To say,
        "Give me eighty men
        and I'll ride through the whole
        Sioux nation."

And there is commander
Carrington, pacing his quarters,
Anxious to stay alive and warm
In this winter chill with premonitions;
A commander possessed,
The fitful hope of arrogance undermined
By the grinding fear that leaps
From the dark of weakness,
Angered by Captain Fetterman who is
Riding even now to the decoys,
Lured behind the ridge he is
Forbidden to cross, led like any
Fool into the trap of one Crazy
Horse, all eighty men in his command
Bushwacked, his own blood flowing
With the blood of all the rest,
Pouring out from the strategy of men
He thought too ignorant
To strategize;
The naked bodies scattered down the hill
under the new falling snow,
Harbingers of other hills to come . . .

And see below us
Crazy Horse, American Horse,
Sitting Bull, Little Horn
Raging across these streams,
Red Cloud and Gall—
The Sioux whose names we all
Will come to know or fear,
Crying for a vision
On these high plains and rivers;
The Cheyennes—
Dull Knife, Little Wolf,
Brave Wolf and Thin Elk,
All camped beneath us
On the Yellowstone
In the heart of winter;

Black Kettle and Left Hand waiting
For Chivington to ride
Out of white hate and ambition
To slaughter the old women
And the children waiting
In the late November sunrise;

Small Woman and Pretty Walker,
Hat Creek miles away behind them,
Gully filling with Cheyenne
Blood and bodies,
Wounded Knee still ahead for some,
Just over the horizon
Of your mind.

You can see this conflict coming;
It tears the ancient grammas
Like a ploughshare,
The deep steel scouring in me,
Tearing us all apart,
And you can hear, under the prairie wind,
The poet's voice:

> "Over pieces of land they are wrangling
> Over iron and oil and fat lands,
> Over breed and kin and race pride . . .
>   And the little wars are leading on
>   into the big war to come."

Watch this conflict with me,
See our agreements broken,
The bonds loosed, cut or torn,
The words unravelling like cobwebs curling
Above the terrible orange perimeter
Under the smoke.

> "Neither fear nor courage saves us,"

Now, says Eliot. In this wild storm

> "Unnatural vices
> Are fathered by our heroism. Virtues
> Are forced upon us by impudent crimes."

Let us speak no more a moment.

My soil is rich enough;
It does not want your blood.

I am Earth, Center,
And Source of all,
But I am only Earth,
And I am stripped by thought
Of this fire coming.

I have no more to give. . . .

LIGHTNING!

"When fear is in their minds,
When pride is woven in the will,
When war is in their hearts,
When they know what they want
And they want their pride kept,
Then, gentlemen, the war will come."
    Carl Sandburg

TESTIMONY of Major S. G. Colley, Indian Agent at Fort Lyon.

Question. Judging from all your information, have you any reason to believe that Black Kettle or Left Hand had been guilty of or intended any hostility toward us?

Answer. I have no reason to believe that of either of them.

Question. Have you any reason to know that they desired to remain at peace?

Answer. Left Hand, who speaks English, told me he would never fight the whites. . . . He was fired on at Fort Larned. He said, "I was not much mad . . . I will not fight the whites and you cannot make me do it. You may imprison me or kill me, but I will not fight the whites."

Question. What was the feeling of Black Kettle?

Answer. He himself always appeared to be friendly.

Question. Did you ever know of his committing an act of hostility towards the whites, or sanctioning it in others?

Answer. I never did.

SECOND REPORT of Colonel Chivington.

General:
    "On 20th of November I left Denver . . . and on 24th of November
    joined with and took command in person of the
    expedition . . . proceeded in a northeasterly direction
    traveling all night, and at daylight on the 29th of November
    striking Sand Creek about forty (40) miles from Fort
    Lyon. . . . The attack was immediately made."

The Indians numbering nine hundred (900)
Or one thousand (1000)
Though taken by surprise
Speedily rallied and formed

A line of battle across the creek
Stubbornly contesting
Every inch of ground.
The engagement became general,
We constantly driving the Indians
Who fell back from one position
To another, for five miles . . .

It may, perhaps, be unnecessary for me
To state that I captured no prisoners.
Between five and six hundred Indians
Were left dead upon the field.

My loss was eight (8) killed
On the field and forty (40)
Wounded, two of which
Have since died.

Night coming on,
Pursuit was of necessity abandoned.

"If all the companies of the 1st Cavalry of Colorado
and the 11th Ohio volunteer cavalry stationed at camps
and posts near here, were ordered to report to me, I
could organize a campaign, which, in my judgement,
would effectively rid the country of these red rebels.

"I am, General, very respectfully, your obedient servant,

J. M. CHIVINGTON"

TESTIMONY of Captain S. M. Robbins, Captain 1st Colorado Cavalry.

By Mr. Gooch:
Question. Were they on that military reservation when this attack was
made on them?

Answer. No, sir. I suppose it was found inconvenient to have so many
of them in the vicinity of the post, on account of their natural thieving
propensities, and they were ordered off on this Sand Creek, about 35
miles from the Fort, on their own reservation, where they could hunt.

Question. They were where they had been directed by the military
authorities to go?

Answer. So I understand. . . . For the information of the committee I
should like to say a friendly word, under the circumstances, in the
Chivington interest. . . . The point I wish to make is, that perhaps
Colonel Chivington might have been forced into this by the sentiment
of the people.

Question. Would the sentiment of the people lead a man to attack Indians who were known to be friendly and who were known to be trying to avert hostilities?

Answer. I should say it would. They want some Indians killed; whether friendly or not they did not stop long to inquire.

TESTIMONY of Major Scott J. Anthony, 1st Colorado Cavalry.

Question. You say you did not approve of the attack upon them by Colonel Chivington. Did you remonstrate with Colonel Chivington against making the attack?

Answer. I did. I made a great many harsh remarks in regard to it. At the same time I did not much object to the killing of Indians as a matter of principle—merely as a matter of policy. I considered it very bad policy as it would open up the war in that whole country again, which was very quiet at the time.

SECOND REPORT of Colonel Shoup, Commanding 3rd Colorado Cavalry.

Dear Sir: I have the honor to report the part taken by my regiment . . .

I was brought into action at sunrise. The first order was . . . to cut off the Indians from their ponies. This order was obeyed with great celerity and success.

. . . I am satisfied, from my own observations, that the historian will search in vain for braver deeds than were committed on that field of battle.

I am sir, with great respect, your obedient servant,

GEORGE F. SHOUP

REPORT of Lieutenant Colonel Bowen.

Sir: I have the honor to enclose you the reports . . .

All behaved well,
each vieing with the other
to see who could do
the most injury.

Permit me to congratulate you
upon the signal punishment
meted out to the savages on yesterday.

I cannot speak in terms
of too high praise of all
under my command.

Very respectfully,

LEAVITT L. BOWERS

REPORT of Major Sayr.

Sir: I have the honor to submit . . .

Both officers and men conducted themselves bravely. . . . The
action became general, and lasted from 6:30 A.M., until 1 P.M., when the
companies divided into small squads and went in pursuit of the Indians,
who were now flying in every direction across the plains, and were
pursued until dark.

Hoping the above will meet your approval, I am &c.,

HAL. SAYR

REPORT of Captain Cree.

Sir:

As for bravery . . .
They all behaved well
and won for themselves a name
that will be remembered for ages to come.

I am, Colonel, yours truly,

T. G. CREE

THE ROCKY MOUNTAIN NEWS REPORTS:

THE BATTLE OF SAND CREEK
"Among the brilliant feats of arms in Indian warfare, the
recent campaign of our Colorado volunteers will stand in history
with few rivals, and none to exceed it in final results."

DEPOSITION: James D. Cannon, being duly sworn says:

. . . In going over the battle-ground the next day, I did not see the body
of a man, woman, or child, but was scalped; and in many instances
their bodies were mutilated in the most horrible manner, men, women,
children—privates cut out, &c. I heard one man say that he had cut a

woman's private parts out, and had them for exhibition on a stick; I heard another say that he had cut the fingers off an Indian to get the rings on the hand. According to the best of my knowledge and belief, these atrocities that were committed were with the knowledge of J. M. Chivington, and I do not know of his taking any measures to prevent them. I heard of one instance of a child a few months old being thrown in the feedbox of a wagon, and after being carried some distance, left on the ground to perish. I also heard of numerous instances in which men had cut out the private part of females, and stretched them over the saddle-bows, and wore them over their hats, while riding in the ranks. All these matters were subjects of general conversation. . . .

Sworn and subscribed to this 27th day of January, 1865.

DEPOSITION: W. P. Minton, being duly sworn says:

. . . Colonel J. M. Chivington, on his arrival at the post of Fort Lyon, was aware of the circumstances in regard to these Indians, from the fact that different officers remonstrated with him. . . .

DEPOSITION: S. G. Colley, being duly sworn, on oath deposes:

. . . Colonel Chivington did, on the morning of the 29th of November last, surprise and attack said camp of friendly Indians and massacre a large number of them (mostly women and children), and did allow the troops under his command to mangle and mutilate them in the most horrible manner.

DEPOSITION: David Louderback, Private 1st Colorado Cavalry, and R. W. Clark, citizen, being duly sworn say:

. . . The entire village was composed of not more than 500 souls, two-thirds of which were women and children.

INTERROGATORIES propounded to John M. Chivington by the Joint Committee on the Conduct of the War, and answers thereto.

7th Question. What number of Indians were killed, and what number of the killed were women and what number were children?

Answer. I judge there were five hundred or six hundred Indians killed. . . . Officers who passed over the field report few women or children dead. . . . I myself saw but one woman who had been killed, and one who had hanged herself; I saw no dead children. . . .

8th Question. State, as nearly as you can, the number of Indians that were wounded.

Answer. I do not know that any Indians were wounded that were not killed.

DEPOSITION: Lieutenant Cramer, sworn:

Lieutenant Dunn went to Colonel Chivington and wanted to know if he could kill his prisoner, young Smith. His reply was, "Don't ask me; you know my orders; I want no prisoners." . . . It is a mistake that there were any white scalps found in the village. I saw one, but it was very old, the hair being much faded. I was ordered to burn the village and was through all the lodges. . . .

DEPOSITION: Samuel G. Colley, sworn and examined:

. . . The Indians for a while made some resistance. Some of the chiefs did not raise an arm, but stood there and were shot down. One of them, Black Kettle, raised an American flag and raised a white flag . . .

There was a good deal of misunderstanding among us there . . .Then there is another thing. The people of Colorado are very much down on Indians. As a general thing they want their land. . . .

DEPOSITION: John Smith, interpreter, being duly sworn says:

From my observation I do not think there were over sixty warriors that made any defense. I rode over the field after the slaughter was over and counted sixty to seventy bodies of dead Indians, a large majority of which were women and children. . . .

DEPOSITION: James Olney, 1st Colorado Cavalry, being duly sworn deposes and says:

. . . Saw three squaws and five children, prisoners in charge of some soldiers; that while they were being conducted along, they were approached by Lieutenant Harry Richmond, of the 3rd Colorado Cavalry; that the Lieutenant Richmond thereupon immediately killed and scalped the three women and five children while they were screaming for mercy. . . .

DEPOSITION: Captain L. Wilson, 1st Colorado Cavalry, being duly sworn says:

. . . We received no information that the Indians at Sand Creek were considered under the protection of the government.

DEPOSITION: Pressly Talbot, sworn:

I was at Fort Lyon the day before the battle; I had a conversation with

Major Anthony. He expressed himself glad that we had come, saying
that he would have attacked the Indians himself had he had sufficient
force.

DEPOSITION: Jacob Downing, sworn:

. . . I heard Colonel Chivington ask Major Anthony how the Indians
were. The major said he wished the Colonel would go out and attack
them . . . I saw no one advance a white flag, and I would have if it had
been done . . . I saw no soldier scalp anybody.

DEPOSITION: S. E. Browne, sworn:

. . . I have seen over a hundred scalps in the city and through the
country said to have been taken at Sand Creek; in September or late
August last, I heard Colonel Chivington in a public speech announce
that his policy was "to kill and scalp all, little and big; that nits make
lice."

STATEMENT: Oliver A. Willard.

I am a clergyman of the Methodist Episcopal Church, residing in
Denver. I know Colonel Chivington and Governor Evans. Both are my
friends, and members of my church . . .

STORM

"Hell's executioner
Hath no ears to hear
What vain art can reply . . .
Lord, have mercy on us!"
        Thomas Nash

Flat calm on the prairie,
Sky unmoving as paint,
Air uneasy in its stillness

Faint stir of dust
in the buffalo wallow,
A little swirl rising on the Rosebud
Kicking up as the wind
Increases, clouds forming
Over the Yellowstone,
Coming down the canyons of the Crazies,
Out of the Beartooths, the Big Horns,
Coming together over the prairie, darkening,

Whole sky in upheaval,
Dust settling as the rain begins,
The big drops small explosions becoming audible,
Sound of a million straw brooms
Sweeping the prairie, sweeping us
All together before these awful mountains,
Grass bending, thunder exploding,
Lightning splitting the old cottonwood
On the bank of the wash,
Sparks glowing inside the stump;
Hailstones strafing the low ridges,
Antelope stumbling, falling;
Terror of young ones, bleating,
Berserk, beaten down in the mud,
The roaring across this land striking us,
Pungence of sage rising,
Cold and darkness engulfing us,
Our children down
In a world that will yet consume with fire
After this storm, these other storms
To come,

The People,
Out again and searching
For one another,
For the lost and dead.

PRAIRIE FIRE

P. S. If anything happens to me, I will telegraph.

Your affectionate son,

  C. W. Collins

Sunlight now, after the storm,
Drying the bunch grass, the sage,
The whole prairie under this dry heat
Turning again to tinder,
The sparks in the stump
Bright red drops.

  March 25
  Settlers on Bluff Creek
  are attacked and driven

from their houses.
No official details.

The old cottonwood
Smouldering till the first breath
Of wind, a gray plume of smoke,
An orange shape of leaf
Leaps up

> April 17
> Detachment of Troop H., Third Cavalry
> commanded by Sgt. Glass has a fight.
> One man wounded, ten Indians reported
> dead; twenty-five wounded.

> June 6
> Captain Monahan in pursuit
> of Indians who have murdered
> four citizens near the post,
> follows their trail one hundred
> miles, surprising them
> in a ravine. He kills three,
> wounds eleven, suffers no loss.

Out of the thunder
Sparks glowing in the grass,
In the stump of the dead tree
Orange flames carouse.

> August 10
> After being hospitably fed
> by these farmers
> the Indians attack and rob them,
> brutally outrage the four females
> until insensible, then plunder
> and burn their houses.

> August 10
> On the same day
> two separate attacks are made
> upon the advance and rear guard
> of a column of troops.
> The advance repulses the attack,
> kills two Indians
> with no losses. The rear
> is also successful:
> Ten Indians are killed,

Twelve wounded. One soldier
is killed.

August 12
Indians attempt to stampede
the livestock by a dash into the camp
of General Sully. They are frustrated
in this design, but later attack
the main body of troops. This attack
is repulsed after a severe fight
lasting twelve hours
in which two soldiers are killed,
three wounded.
Twelve Indians are reported killed,
Fifteen wounded.

August 12
The same day
Indians, though kindly received
and fed by the people,
plunder and burn five houses,
steal ten head of stock cattle,
murder fifteen persons,
wound two, outrage five women,
two of whom are also shot.

August 12
The same day
A small band crosses the river
kills two persons there
and returns with two captive
children, named Bell.
Here they again attack the settlers
intending to clear out the valley.
While a Mr. Schmerhorn
is defending his house,
Captain Benteen with his troop
of Seventh Cavalry arrives
to the relief of the house
and runs the Indians about ten miles.
Two women ravished and captured
are rescued.

The brush fires flowing together now
A single line of light, a conflagration
Under the smoke, a foul stratus front, moving.

August 13
General Sully is again attacked;
one soldier is killed, four wounded.
Indians are reported routed
with ten killed, twelve wounded.

August 14
A house is plundered and burned,
one person killed, one wounded.
One woman is outraged and captured.

Other incidents inflame
The clear August air

August ⑱   ⑲   ㉑   ㉒
        ㉓   ㉔   ㉕   ㉗
        ㉘   ㉙   ㉛

Trees braced against this onslaught,
Trunks cracking
Till it seems there
Can be no end
To this hatred . . .

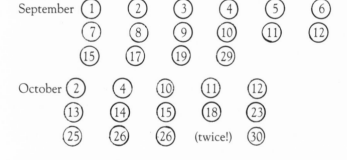

September ①   ②   ③   ④   ⑤   ⑥
          ⑦   ⑧   ⑨   ⑩   ⑪   ⑫
          ⑮   ⑰   ⑲   ㉙

October ②   ④   ⑩   ⑪   ⑫
        ⑬   ⑭   ⑮   ⑱   ㉓
        ㉕   ㉖   ㉖ (twice!) ㉚

Heat so intense
No cold can stop it,
No snow hide the black
Beneath it; Earth scorched and seared
With fire and blood,
Only the wild rose knows
Where this blood dries
On the backs of leaves,
Red drops turning dull
In the fire this heat excites

November
(20) (25)

Fire so hot this sod
Lies warm forever;
Bright lines of flickering pain
Sucking the breath from the lungs
Of antelope leaping in vain
To escape—
Smell of burned flesh,
Heat roaring in our ears

> April 7, 1869
> On the Musselshell River, Montana,
> detachments of D, F, and G Companies
> Thirteenth Infantry, have a fight,
> kill nine Indians, suffer the loss
> of one soldier killed, two wounded.

Reports pour in

> April (16)
> April (20)
> April (22)
> May (2)
> May (10)

Many soldiers falling;
So many soldiers falling
Sitting Bull would dream
Of many soldiers
Falling into camp on the Horn.
Indians falling too,
Green hay in the meadows
Mowed down and left to rot.

May, June, July, August,
The same summer after summer.

August 8 Telegram of Alf. Sully, United States Army, Helena.

". . . there is a white element in this country which, from its rowdy
and lawless character, cannot be excelled in any section, and the traffic
in whisky with Indians in this Territory is carried on to an alarming
extent. This frequently causes altercations between whites and
Indians . . . I intend to do all I can to arrest some of the citizens who,

about ten days ago, committed the cowardly murder of a harmless old man and a boy about fourteen years old, at Fort Benton. They were Piegans. These Indians were shot in broad day-light in the streets of the town. I think I can arrest the murderers, but doubt very much I can convict them in any court . . .

"Nothing can be done to insure peace and order till there is military force here strong enough to clear out the roughs and the whisky in the country."

No troops can be spared
To chastize obstreperous whites
Who murder Indians.

This spark still
Glowing in the dark . . .

August 18 Telegram of General Sully, Helena, Montana.
"Sir: I fear we will have to consider the Blackfeet (Piegans) in a state of war. In addition to the late attack by these Indians on a train near Fort Benton a large number of horses have been stolen within fifty miles of here, and early this morning a ranch twenty-five miles from here was attacked and two men shot. The miners are very much exasperated."

But troops can be found
To chastize Indians,
The spark ablaze, no end
In sight, the prairie charred
Silver black in the moonlight.

"It was therefore resolved . . ."

As soon as winter set in
And the Indians unable to move,
To send a force from Fort Ellis
And

"Strike them a hard blow."

January 23, 1870
After a secret night march
the column, under Major Baker,
completely surrounded and surprised
the camps of Bear Chief and Big Horn,
killing one hundred and seventy three
Indians, wounding twenty additional,
capturing one hundred and forty women

and children, and over three hundred horses.
The village was destroyed,
and the column pushed on downstream
where the lodges of Mountain Chief were found
abandoned. They were burned, the Indians
having scattered in every direction.

February 6
The column reached Fort Ellis today,
having marched six hundred miles
in the coldest weather known for years
in the always severe climate of this region.
One white man was killed.

The fire in winter!
Never out, the snow afire,
The cold aflame.
The following summer the same . . .

1872
August 14
Pryor's Fork, Montana,
several hundred Sioux and Cheyenne
attack a column of Second Cavalry
and Seventh Infantry . . .

August 17
Yellowstone River, Montana
one man of Troop L, Second Cavalry
is wounded in a skirmish.

August 18
Mouth of Powder River, Montana,
Companies D, F, and G, Twenty-Second Infantry
fight with Indians.

August 21
The same troops are again engaged.

August 22
The same troops engaged once more
on O'Fallon's Creek, Montana.

And the little wars leading on
into the big war still to come . . .

Years of blood and fire
Flowing over this prairie,

Antelope kids bleating,
Smoke choking us,
Drawing us into a firestorm
To learn again
Under all the divisions,

    "The faces of Cain and Abel in each of us,"

Become the suffering face of Job.
Custer and Sitting Bull
Related
Custer and Sitting Bull
One!

FIRESTORM

*"These men fought in any case
and some believing . . ."*
    Ezra Pound

June, 1876
You can see
From this high place
How it was along the Yellowstone
Just a week after Crook
Was sent running from the Rosebud,
Whipped by the Sioux —
Almost a family outing:
George Armstrong Custer,
Puffed up again by command;
His brother Tom, fierce soldier,
Holder of two Congressional
Medals of Honor;
Their brother Boston Custer,
A civilian along for his health;
Brother-in-law Lieutenant James Calhoun;
And Autie Reed, nephew and
Favorite of Libby Custer.
His death would be almost
As great a blow to her
As the death of her husband.

And you can see Terry,
Gibbon and Custer meeting
On the Far West to plan their strategy,

Then watch them part;
Terry and Gibbon to continue
Up the Yellowstone
Then swing south along the Big Horn,
Custer moving south
Along the Rosebud.
They plan to rendezvous
On the Little Big Horn
And somewhere in that country
Enclose the hostiles,
Coming upon them from two directions
And able to support one another
In the attack.

Their plan is simple,
Open to revision by events in the field,
And could be effective.
But you can also see
Down there
Where Custer runs
Into a large force of hostiles
In the valley of the Little Big Horn
And divides his troops.

He sends Benteen off to the left
To test how far south the village
Might extend along the river
And cut off escape in that direction.
He sends Reno down from the hills
To attack the village
From the river bottom. From there
Reno will ride downstream into the teepees
And Custer will come to his support
From the east, striking the village
In the middle or from above.

But there are trees
And swamps and Indians
In the bottom.
Reno's charge breaks around them;
He forms a skirmish line
Which does not hold,
Then retreats in disorder
Across the river.
Men drown there like buffalo

Crossing; they thrash in the swarm
Of comrades and horses and swirling currents,
Terror and Indians, Indians
Cutting men down in the river,
Indians already in the gullies and ravines,
All along the bluffs the soldiers seek
As refuge.

Custer tries to come in from the east,
Is forced back,
Racing for high ground
Where his last combat closes around him
Like a night flower folding in;
No time for one last letter to Libby,
No words, singing in the mind.

Reno pulls his troops together
On the bluffs, and is joined by Benteen
Who has wasted an hour, his horses at a walk.
On the ridge where they think Custer to be
They hear heavy firing
But can not or will not,
Do not, go to his assistance.
They are besieged by thousands of Indians
Throughout the afternoon, that night
And through the next day.

The following noon
Terry and Gibbon arrive
Two days late
And a command short.

GENERAL CUSTER'S CHECKBOOK

Drawn on the First National Bank of St. Paul:

> # 5
> _____
> Date: *May 11, 1876*
> _____
> To: *John B. Putts*
> _____
> *Premium Life Assurances*
> _____
> *Equitable ins.* Amt. *$46.70*

> # 14
> _____
> Date: *May 18, 1876*
> _____
> To: *Life Ass'n of America*
> _____
> *Premium ins.*
> _____
> *Life Policy until Dec. '76* Amt. *$ 210.00*

SITTING BULL TALKS
TO THE NEW YORK HERALD
NOVEMBER 17, 1877

Your people look up to men
Because they are rich,
Because they have much land,
Many lodges and many women.
I suppose
My people look up to me
Because I am poor.
This is the difference between us.

Some whites say
A time will come
With no buffalo,
But those are the words
Of an American
And therefore cannot
Be taken as true.

It is strange:
Americans complain
We kill buffaloes.
We kill buffaloes
As we kill other animals,
For food and clothing
And to make our lodges warm.
They kill buffaloes
For what?
Go through your country,
See the carcasses rotting.
Your young men shoot for pleasure;
They take a tail or tongue,
The head or horns,
To prove they killed.
What is this?
Is it robbery?
You call us savages.
What are they?
They are barbarians.

When I was not yet born,
When I was not yet in my mother's arms
But in her belly,

It was there I began
To study about my people.
I studied there
In the womb,
About many things—
The smallpox killing my people.
I was so interested
I turned over on my side.
Wakan-Tanka must have told me
At that time
I would be the one
To be the judge of all the Indians,
To decide for them
In all their ways.

I never taught my people
To trust Americans.
I have told them the truth—
That the Americans are great
Liars. I never treated with them
In a way to surrender my people's
Rights. I traded,
But always gave full value
For what I got.

I fought.
But not until after
I had tried hard not to fight.

ON THE HILL
WITH CUSTER

Sheridan. (Lieutenant General P. H., Department of the Missouri)

"Precisely what was done by Custer's
immediate command, subsequent to the moment
when the rest of the regiment last saw him
alive, has remained partly a matter of conjecture,
no officer or soldier who rode
with him into the valley of the Little Big
Horn having lived to tell the tale. The
only real evidence of how they came to meet
their fate was the testimony of the field
where it overtook them."

Yellow Horse. (Hostile. Sioux)

The hills were covered by swallows
Diving in every direction.
The Indians were going in every direction
Like myriads of swallows
Yet the great body
All the time
Moving down on Custer.

Edgerly. (Winfield S., 2nd Lieutenant, D Company)

General Custer and his brother Tom,
And Cooke, were at the top of the ridge.

Only a few men on the hill
Were scalped since they all got short
Haircuts before we started.
Crittendon was stuck full of arrows.
Calhoun's men were in good line
With the officers, where they should have been
To offer good resistance.

Gall. (Hostile. Chief of the Hunkpapa Sioux)

The first two companies,
Keogh and Calhoun,
Dismounted and fought on foot.
They never broke
But retired step by step
Until forced back to the ridge
Where they all perished.
They were shot down in line
Where they stood.

De Rudio. (Charles. First Lieutenant, E Company)

First man we found was
Butler, neither stripped nor scalped.

I counted 214 dead on the field,
Custer up on top the knoll,
Five or six horses around
Like they'd been led there
And shot. The horses all sorrels
From Company C.

There was a gully on one side
Full of dead men.

Lieutenant Riley,
Whom I liked,
Lay near Custer and was
Full of arrows.

    Red Horse. (Hostile. Sioux)

    We swarmed down upon them
    And drove them before us
    In confusion.
    They were panic-stricken;
    Some threw down their arms
    And threw up their hands.

    No prisoners were taken,
    All were killed,
    None left alive even for
    A few minutes.

Hare. (Luther. 2nd Lieutenant, detached to Varnum)

I saw the horses.
Some said they were shot
To make breastworks
But they were poorly arranged
And I think they were just killed
The way they were killed.
Crittendon had an arrow
In the eye. Tom Custer
Was all cut up and mutilated,
But they did not cut out
His heart. Cooke had a sideburn
Cut off, but no one was scalped.

    Low Dog. (Hostile. Sioux)

    Everything was in confusion
    All the time of the fight.
    I did not see General Custer;
    I do not know who killed him.
    We did not know till the fight was over
    That he was the white chief.

    If Reno and his warriors
    Had fought as Custer
    And his warriors fought
    The battle might have been
    Against us.

Knipe. (Also Kanipe. Daniel A., enlisted)

Christ what a sight!
Every man stripped,
Most had hatchet blows
Across the forehead.
Custer had only one wound—
Through the chest.
I got a good look at him,
Lying with the small
Of his back across
Another dead soldier,
And I may say
Any who said
He was shot in the head
Or had powder burns
Is a liar for sure.
I missed Tom Custer,
My own Captain, somehow,
But the bodies were badly
Bloated after two days
In the hot sun.

I walked along one gulch
And counted 28 bodies in there
Including Mitch's.
At least I'm sure in my own
Mind, it was Mitch,
But I didn't climb down in
To see.

I can't recall mutilations
Except to bring death to the wounded.
This was generally accomplished
By chopping open the head
Across the eyes.

> *Hump.* (Hostile. Sioux)
>
> Long Haired Chief and his men
> Became confused.
> They retreated slowly
> But it was no time
> Till we had them surrounded.
> Then we made such short work
> of killing them

That no man could give
A correct account of it.

Adams. (Jacob. Enlisted)

We found old Comanche
Sitting on his haunches,
Front feet all braced, holding him up.
We got him up and he just
Followed us around.

I helped bury all those bodies
On the west slope,
And E Troop over near the gully,
Then took sick to my stomach
From the stench
And went to the river
To get a drink.
Down in the river bottom
Lieutenant Gibson and I
Found Mac's body. The Indians
Had fired the grass and Mac
Was scorched.
The Lieutenant wanted me to get a mule
And pack Mac up Reno Hill,
But I disliked that job
And told him I knew no way
To pick it up
Without it coming to pieces,
So he said bury it here and left.

But I just left Mac there.
What the hell.

    Wooden Leg. (Hostile. Cheyenne)

    Our warriors surrounded them.
    As we closed in
    The soldiers began to shoot
    Each other, and to shoot
    Themselves.
    I rode to the eastern end
    Of the ridge,
    But the soldiers there
    Were dead also.

    Not all the soldiers
    Had died right away.

One, a captain, still lived.
He was dazed, but raised up
On an elbow, glaring wildly
At us. We fell back
Amazed, thinking perhaps
He had returned from the spirit world.
A Sioux finally
took the revolver from the man's hand
And shot him through the head.
He was the last to die.
We do not know who he was.

Martin. (John. Trumpeter, Orderly for Custer)

We marked Custer's grave.
Lieutenant Wallace wrote his name
On a piece of paper, rolled it up
And stuck it in an empty,
Then put it near a little stake
I drove by Custer's head.

    Two Moon. (Hostile. Cheyenne)

    We circle all around them
    Swirling like water
    Around a stone.
    We shoot,
    We ride fast,
    We shoot again!

    Soldiers drop,
    Horses fall on them!

    One man
    Rides up and down the line
    All the time shouting.
    He rode a sorrel horse
    With white face
    And white fore-legs.
    I don't know who he was.
    He was a very brave man.
    The man on the sorrel horse led some
    Brave men, and helped them remain brave.
    He wore a buckskin shirt,
    Had long black hair and mustache.
    He fought hard with a big knife.
    His men were white with dust.

The Sioux said the other man
With the mustache was Long Hair
The big chief. I do not know.
I had never seen him.
The man on the white-faced horse—
That was the bravest man.

Foley. (John. Company K. Enlisted)
I went to the village site
In the river bottom;
Scuffling along I kicked over
A big kettle.
The red-haired head of the corporal
From G Troop
Was under it.

   Sitting Bull. (Hostile. Sioux)

These men fought
over there on the hillside,
many young men are missing from our lodges,
but—
Is there an American wife
who has her husband left?

I tell no lies about dead men.
These men were as good men
as ever fought. They fired on us
with needle guns;
we replied with magazine guns.

When the Long Hair found
he was so outnumbered
he took the best course.
All the men fell back fighting
and dropping.
They could not fire fast enough.

I have talked with people;
I cannot find one who saw
Long Hair till just before he died.
He did not wear his hair long
as he used to wear it.
It was short; the color of grass
when the frost comes.

He killed a man when he fell.
He laughed.

I said he laughed. He fired
his last shot from his pistol,
and he laughed.
After he fell he rose up
on his hands and tried
another shot, but
his pistol would not go off.

I did not see it;
I was told it,
but it is true.

The Little Big Horn
June 25, 1876
10:00 P.M.

My Dear Elizabeth,

It is cold here now. The sun has gone and the night has set in. I miss you terribly this evening. Though surrounded by my comrades, brave troopers all, it is so still I think I can hear your heart beating to me across the plains. Nevertheless, I am glad you are not here, but safe at Lincoln. I hope Reno comes soon; the rain is so cold on this hillside you cannot imagine; yet I know tomorrow the heat again will be intense.

You will hear the news of today's debacle soon enough. I only regret the swirl of painful controversy that will ensue upon publication of these events, and pray you strength to continue to believe the best of me. Our old enemies will strive again to make me out a fool or disobedient; a trial you are by now accustomed to. Perhaps history will foil them again.

Believe whatever I did was done for purpose. It seemed clear at the time. That it should come to this sad end could not be forseen. Enough. You have been my companion and comfort all along. Now you are even more important to me, for the separation from you which this new duty entails seems unendurable.

Forgive my foolishness. Remember me as one who loved you, and would gladly die again to spare you this embarrassment and pain. I do not know where Autie is, I could not keep trace near the end. Tom is here with me, lying just above; Boston also, a few yards below. They look so pale in this thin light. They fought well and send their love, as do I—

Your devoted husband,

[signature: G. A. Custer]

George A. Custer

XI. EMBERS

W hen that day comes, that you sit down
broken, without one human creature to
whom you cling, with your loves the dead and
the living dead . . . when in the present there is
no craving and in the future no hope, then, oh,
with a beneficent tenderness, Nature enfolds
you."
     Olive Schreiner
     The Story of an African Farm

F or what can be expected of beings in such a
situation as we are?. . . The appropriate
form of address between man and man ought to
be, not Sir, but fellow sufferer . . . it cor-
responds to the true nature of the case, makes
us see other men in a true light and reminds us
of what are the most necessary of all things:
tolerance, patience, forbearance and charity,
which each of us needs, and which each of us
therefore owes."
     Arthur Schopenauer
     "On the Suffering of the World"

T he life of fire comes from the death of
earth. The life of air comes from the death
of fire. The life of water comes from the death
of air. The life of earth comes from the death
of water."
     Herakleitos
     fragment 34

A fter such knowledge, what forgiveness?"
T. S. Eliot
     "Gerontion"

EMBERS

"Whatever we inherit from the fortunate
We have taken from the defeated
What they had to leave us — a symbol:
A symbol perfected in death."
          T. S. Eliot

Now
In the dark
The rain comes again,
The wet redemption of the just
And the unjust,
          "A tempest of rain came;
          the night was black as ink,"
   John Martin said,
Washing the blood from the naked men
Exhausted of their lives, stripped
In their final instant of eyes
Flaring widely just before the dark;
The last few embers turning
Into the darkness of Earth,
The darkness
Where we wander still
Alien from our own time and place.
Rivers no longer part
For us;
Highways are not built straight
For us in the wilderness.
Our mutual past,
The Promethean rock
To which we are bound;
Our anxious present,
The turbulent swift terror
Of birds, swept-winged
And silver in the sun;
All the reciprocity of our days
Flowing in us, a river,
Yellowstone or Rosebud . . .

So now
I call you back to me
And to this high place
On Rampart Range,
That from this distance
In this new day
We may see again
The inexorable and the ephemeral
In face of which we choose
Our life; our being *for*
Or being *against*, the *being*
For which we are willing to stand,
And failing,
To stand and try once more.
    And though too late to cleanse
Or once again make whole
That which we have broken
        The word
        The lives
We have broken again and again,
I put these plains and rivers
Before us
That we may see
    South of us
Black Kettle dead on the Washita
In the dead of a winter dawn,
Custer and the 7th
Riding out of the snow
From all sides, killing
As many as they can,
Warriors and women falling dead at daybreak,
    And we can see north of us
Little Wolf buried —
Propped upright on the hill
Beyond the Big Horns,
Stones dragged up by travois,
Piled over his face —
Little Wolf stands in the rock
Watching his people still,
    And Roman Nose
Six foot three inches in height,
Two hundred fifty pounds in weight,
Muscled like his war pony,
Painted to match his skill and daring

He rode untouched
By arrows or bullets
Victory after victory.
  He had an agreement with metal:
      "If I do not touch
        your flesh, Iron, before I fight,
        you will not touch mine."
The agreement held,
Till at Beecher's Island
A woman who did not know
Served him food stirred
With a metal spoon.
There was no time for ceremony,
No ritual of purification.
That afternoon metal
Touched him,
The lead slug blossoming inside,
Filling his chest with sleep;
  And Crazy Horse,
Called the Light-Haired Boy,
Born in the fall
Of the Year the Oglalla Stole One Hundred Horses,
Now fallen forever
In a welter of deceit
At Fort Robinson,
Lied to by General Miles,
His arms pinned by his old friend
Little Big Man, one of his own
Tribe running the cool blade
Of the bayonet through his side
So smoothly it only drew
A sudden inhaling under
The startled eyes
A minute before the pain began.
He lingered a few hours,
Before he died said to his father,
      "Father, it is no use to depend on me. . . ."
  They are all here now,
Have had their day
And lost it.
      "They talk now in their last sleep,"
  Sandburg says,
Their names cracking the silence
As the ground cracks

Open, trembling for the future
After drought, or quake;
The names clamoring still
In the names of small towns
Or schools—Custer, Terry,
Sheridan and Lame Deer—
All gone now,
No one to answer to the names;
Bridger gone under,
Portuguese Phillips gone,
Home at last
After the long ride,
Fetterman sleeping still
On Lodge Trail Ridge,
Reno cowering on his bluffs,
Everyone gathered here now
Under my hills and rivers,
All the old names still
Alive and awfully quiet,
Circling . . .

Kearney, Harney,
Carrington and Laramie;
John Martin, who became
A ticket chopper
At the Hundred and Third Street
Subway station in New York;
   John M. Chivington, back in Denver
For the great reunion,
The terror of Cheyenne children
Only a pain-bathed memory of fear
In the minds of the survivors,
Now middle-aged, defeated and demeaned;
The colonel still straight and proud,
Smiling and bowing
Before the tumultuous ovation;
I have him now too.
   And old Joseph,
Driving up the Clark Fork
Just down there—
Crossing the Yellowstone
At Laurel, reaching the Bear Paws,
Fighting until he can fight
No more, forever.

American Horse
Walking out of his cave
On the arms of his warriors,
Holding in his intestines
Where he has been shot
Through the abdomen, quietly
Exchanging greetings with Crook,
Then walking to the little fire of his people
Never uttering a complaint,
Refusing aid when the army doctors offered,
Telling his friends,
        "I want to die . . ."
He died before morning.
  Sitting Bull
Gone under as well;
Down from Canada,
Brought to the post
By a ruse;
What could not be won
With honor, won by deception,
One of his own holding the gun
That brought him
Crashing down,
An old tree, fallen
To nourish the roots
Of the short grass
And sleep within my breast.
  All the warriors gone under now,
Wrapped in the vast silence,
In time, the river,
Taking them under,
Under the sage brush and the sand,
Their bones bleached and blown to dust
Drowning in the light.

XII. POSTLUDE

O*f all that was done in the past*
you eat the fruit, either rotten or ripe."
T. S. Eliot
Choruses from "The Rock"

F*ew of us have the heart to follow the circle*
to the end."
John Updike
"The Music Room"

O*f the dead who really live, whose presence*
we know, we hardly care to speak — we
know their hush."
D. H. Lawrence
Selected Letters

N*obody knows what the soil is, except that*
it is something working towards a
balance, something that balances itself with
death as well as life, and needs long years to do
so."
Haniel Long
If He Can Make Her So

CONTEXTS:
CHANT THE SACRED CIRCLE

Now
From this high place
See
Beyond the markers
Of men from Little Big Horn,
The neat rows of government graves
White and gleaming
Under the pines, soughing
In this eternal wind;

Beyond the unknown graves
Of warriors from Sand Creek
And Hat Creek,
Indian voices keening on the fragile air,

Lift your eyes to see
     pine ridges and deer
     sage brush along the Tongue
     the ghosts of buffalo
     and bone pickers
     the sun a cataract through the clouds

And beyond the limit of the eye
     another sun behind the sun we know
     and other suns in time
     and stars
     and Blackfeet warriors on painted horses
     raiding the darkness out there
     beyond the black holes
     and warriors older than any of our kind
     riding through time
     mounted on flame-maned stallions
     scattering suns as they ride through
     the white holes

                          out there

Beyond all the suns and all
The darkness, the galaxies
Beyond penetration by light or mind

Out there—

> the pulse
> numbers, ordering themselves in time
> music
> circling back
> knitting all together
> this Earth
> this small heart
> an exhausted antelope
> a quicksilver spring in the dark hills
> the first word
> and the last word
> the same:

> The People

> drinking compassion
> after the hard run
> the long pursuit

SOURCES QUOTED

I. PRELUDE

Davenport, Guy. *Herakleitos and Diogenes.* San
  Francisco, 1979.
Eliot, T. S. *Selected Poems.* New York, 1964.
Kirk, G. S., and Raven, J. E. *The Presocratic Philosophers.*
  Cambridge, 1957.
Lombardo, Stanley. *Parmenides and Empedocles: The
  Fragments in Verse Translation.* San Francisco, 1982.
The Upanishads. Translated by Juan Marasco. New York,
  1965.

II. CHANT THE CREATION

Alt, David D., and Hyndman, Donald W. *Roadside
  Geology of the Northern Rockies.* Missoula, 1974.
Clark, Grahame. *World Prehistory: An Outline.*
  Cambridge, 1962.
Cook, Charles W.; Folsom, David E.; and Peterson,
  William. *The Valley of the Upper Yellowstone.* Edited by
  Aubrey L. Haines. Norman, 1965.
Eggan, Frederick. From a speech. Sun Valley, Idaho,
  1980.
Eliot, T. S. *Four Quartets.* New York, 1943.
Hamilton, W. T. *My Sixty Years on the Plains, Trapping,
  Trading, and Indian Fighting.* Norman, 1960.
Kirk, G. S., and Raven, J. E. *The Presocratic Philosophers.*
  Cambridge, 1957.
Lombardo, Stanley. *Parmenides and Empedocles: The
  Fragments in Verse Translation.* San Francisco, 1982.

Ojakangas, Richard W., and Darby, David G. *The Earth
    Past and Present.* New York, 1976.
Russell, Osborne. *Journal of a Trapper, 1834-1843.*
    Edited by Aubrey L. Haines. Lincoln, 1955.
Seneca. *Letters from a Stoic.* New York, 1969.
Shanker, David S.; Tiffney, Bruce H. and Wing, Scott.
    The Age of Mammals. New Haven, 1978.
Wormington, H. M. *Ancient Man in North America.*
    Denver, 1957.

III. WE ARE ALL RELATED

Aurelius, Marcus. *Meditations.* Baltimore, 1964.
Brown, Joseph Epes. *The Sacred Pipe.* Norman, 1953.
Catlin, George. *Letters and Notes on the Manners,
    Customs, and Conditions of North American Indians.* New
    York, 1973.
Denig, Edwin Thompson. *Five Indian Tribes of the
    Upper Missouri.* Norman, 1961.
_____*46th Annual Report to the American
    Bureau of Ethnology.* Washington, D. C., 1928.
Engler, George. Personal conversation. Red Lodge, 1959.
Ewers, John C. *The Horse in Blackfoot Indian Culture.*
    Washington, D. C., 1955.
Grinnell, George B. *Blackfoot Lodge Tales, The Story of a
    Prairie People.* Lincoln, 1962.
Hoebel, E. Adamson. *The Cheyennes, Indians of the
    Great Plains.* New York, 1960.
Kane, Paul. *Paul Kane's Frontier.* Edited by J. Russell
    Harper. Fort Worth, 1971.
La Roque, François. *Journal of François La Roque from
    the Assiniboin River to the Yellowstone – 1805.* Missoula,
    no date.
Linderman, Frank B. *Plenty-Coups, Chief of the Crows.*
    Lincoln, 1962.
Lombardo, Stanley, *Parmenides and Empedocles: The
    Fragments in Verse Translation.* San Francisco, 1982.
Lowie, Robert. *Indians of the Plains.* Garden City, 1954.
_____*The Crow Indians.* New York, 1965.
Saum, Lewis O. *The Fur Trader and the Indian.* Seattle,
    1965.
Seger, John H. *Early Days Among the Cheyenne and
    Arapahoe Indians.* Bloomington, 1968.
Swanton, John R. *The Indian Tribes of North America.*
    Washington, D. C., 1952.

IV. SO VAGRANT A CONDITION

Clark, William, and Lewis, Meriweather. *The Journals of Lewis and Clark*. Edited by Reuben Gold Thwaites. New York, 1959.

Cox, Ross. *Journals of David Thompson*. Edited by M. Catherine White. Missoula, 1950. See below.

Elliott, Lawrence. *The Long Hunter*. New York, 1976.

Ferris, W. A. *Life in the Rocky Mountains, 1830-1835*. Denver, 1940.

Field, Harry. Personal conversation. Red Lodge, 1958.

Larpenteur, Charles. *Forty Years a Fur Trader on the Upper Missouri, 1833-1872*. Edited by Elliott Coues. New York, 1898.

Leonard, Zenas. *Narrative of the Adventures of Zenas Leonard*. Ann Arbor, 1966.

McDonnell, John. *Journals of David Thompson*. Edited by M. Catherine White. Missoula, 1950. See below.

Marcy, Randolph Barnes. *The Prairie Traveler*. Williamstown, 1968.

Myers, John Myers. *The Saga of Hugh Glass*. Lincoln, 1953.

Pattie, James Ohio. *The Personal Narrative of James O. Pattie of Kentucky*. Cincinnati, 1931.

Ross, Alexander. *Journals of David Thompson*. Edited by M. Catherine White. Missoula, 1950. See below.

Russell, Osborne. *Journal of a Trapper, 1834-1843*. Edited by Aubrey L. Haines. Lincoln, 1955.

Thompson, David. *David Thompson's Journals Relating to Montana and Adjacent Regions, 1808-1812*. Edited by M. Catherine White. Missoula, 1950.

Vestal, Stanley, *Jim Bridger, Mountain Man*. Lincoln, 1970.

Victor, Frances Fuller. *The River of the West*. Columbus, 1950.

V. WEST OF MISSOURI

Delano, A. *Life on the Plains and Among the Diggings*. Buffalo, 1854.

Hulbert, Archer Butler. *Forty-Niners, the Chronicle of the California Trail*. Boston, 1932.

Miller, James Knox Polk. *The Road to Virginia City: The Diary of James Knox Polk Miller*. Edited by Andrew F. Rolle. Norman, 1960.

Noble, A. G. Unpublished diary. Denver, 1863.

Pigman, Walter Griffith. *The Journal of Walter Griffith Pigman.* Edited by Ulla Staley Fawkes. Mexico, Mo. 1942.

Pritchard, James A. *The Overland Diary of James A. Pritchard from Kentucky to California in 1849.* Edited by Dale L. Morgan. San Francisco, 1959.

VI. THE TREE

Davenport, Guy. *Herakleitos and Diogenes.* San Francisco, 1979.

De Chardin, Teilhard. *Hymn to the Universe.* London, 1965.

Eliot, T. S. *Selected Poems.* New York, 1964.

VII. THE LITANY OF THE BUFFALO

Brown, Mark, and Felton, W. R. *The Frontier Years.* New York, 1955.

Dary, David. *The Buffalo Book.* New York, 1974.

Haines, Frances, *The Buffalo.* New York, 1970.

McHugh, Tom. *The Time of the Buffalo.* New York, 1972.

Russell, Charles M. *Trails Plowed Under.* New York, 1927.

Russell, Osborne, *Journal of a Trapper, 1834-1843.* Edited by Aubrey L. Haines. Lincoln, 1955.

Sandoz, Mari. *The Buffalo Hunters.* Lincoln, 1958.

Stuart, Granville. *Pioneering in Montana.* Lincoln, 1977.

Townsend, John Kirk. *Narrative of a Journey Across the Rocky Mountains to the Columbia River.* Lincoln, 1978.

VIII. SOUND OF THE SNAPPING GUIDON

Bourke, John B. *Mackenzie's Last Fight with the Cheyennes.* Ann Arbor, 1966.

——————————*On the Border with Crook.* Lincoln, 1961.

Finerty, John R. *War-Path and Bivouac.* Norman, 1961.

Frontier. "Seven Letters from Wyoming Territory, 1870-1871." *Annals of Wyoming.* Cheyenne, 1978.

King, Charles, *Campaigning with Crook.* Norman, 1964.

Knight, Oliver. *Life and Manners in the Frontier Army.* Norman, 1978.

Nevin, David. *The Soldiers.* New York, 1973.

Rickey, Don. *Forty Miles a Day on Beans and Hay.*
　　Norman, 1963.
Ryan, John. Unpublished letter. Custer Archives,
　　Billings.
Seneca. *Letters from a Stoic.* New York, 1959.
Utley, Robert M. *Frontier Regulars, the United States
　　Army and the Indian, 1866-1890.* New York, 1973.
　　——————————*Frontiersman in Blue: The United
　　States Army and the Indian, 1848-1865.* New York, 1967.
Whitman, S. E. *The Troopers, an Informal History of the
　　Plains Cavalry, 1865-1890.* New York, 1962.
Report of the General of the Army, 1866.
Report of the Secretary of War, 1876.
Senate Executive Document #15, 2nd Session, 39th
　　Congress, Vol. 1277.

IX. REPORT OF THE COMMISSION

Cicero. *Selected Works.* New York, 1960.
Davenport, Guy. *Herakleitos and Diogenes.* San
　　Francisco, 1979.
Fourth Annual Report of the Board of Indian
　　Commissioners to the President of the United States,
　　1872. Washington, D. C., 1872.
Marcy, Randolph Barnes. *The Prairie Traveler.*
　　Williamstown, 1968.

X. PRAIRIE FIRE

Aurelius, Marcus. *Meditations.* Baltimore, 1964.
Camp, Walter. *Custer in '76.* Provo, 1976.
Commissioner of Indian Affairs, *Annual Report, 1870.*
　　Washington, D. C., 1870.
Custer, George A. *My Life on the Plains.* Lincoln, 1966.
Eliot, T. S. *The Waste Land and Other Poems.* New York,
　　1962.
Finerty, John F. *War-Path and Bivouac.* Norman, 1961.
Graham, W. A., *The Custer Myth, A Sourcebook of
　　Custeriana.* New York, 1953.
House Executive Documents #185, #197, 2nd Session,
　　41st·Congress, 1870.
Lewis, Sol. *The Sand Creek Massacre, A Documentary
　　History.* New York, 1973.
Lombardo, Stanley. *Parmenides and Empedocles: The
　　Fragments in Verse Translation.* San Francisco, 1982.

Nash, Thomas. Quoted in _Poetry, Theory and Practice_.
   Edited by Laurence Perrine. New York, 1952.
Pound, Ezra. _Cantos_. New York, 1967.
Reznikoff, Charles. Testimony: Volume One, The United
   States 1885-1915. Santa Barbara, 1978.
Ricker, Eli Seavey. The Ricker Collection. Nebraska
   Historical Society Archives. Lincoln.
Sandburg, Carl. _Breathing Tokens_. New York, 1978.
Secretary of War. _Annual Report, 1870_. Washington, D.
   C., 1870.
Senate Executive Document #49, 2nd Session, 41st
   Congress, 1870.
Spring, Agnes Wright. _Caspar Collins, The Life and
   Exploits of an Indian Fighter of the Sixties_. Lincoln, 1969.
U.S. Government Printing Office. _Record of Engagements
   with Hostile Indians from 1868-1882_. Washington, D. C.,
   1882.

XI. EMBERS

Davenport, Guy. _Herakleitos and Diogenes_. San
   Francisco, 1979.
Eliot, T. S. _Four Quartets_. New York, 1943.
_____The Waste Land and Other Poems_.
   New York, 1962.
Ricker, Eli Seavey. The Ricker Collection. Nebraska
   Historical Society Archives. Lincoln.
Sandburg, Carl. _Breathing Tokens_. New York, 1978.
Schopenhauer, Arthur. _Essays and Aphorisms_. New York,
   1970.
Schreiner, Olive. _The Story of an African Farm_. New
   York, 1939.

XII. POSTLUDE

Eliot, T. S. _Selected Poems_. New York, 1964.
Lawrence, D. H. _Selected Letters_. New York, 1978.
Long, Haniel. _If He Can Make Her So_. Pittsburgh, 1968.
Updike, John. "The Music Room." _The Great American
   Short Story_. New York, 1977.